YOUNG RIDER'S HANDBOOK

CARE AND FITNESS

JO BIRD

YOUNG RIDER'S HANDBOOK

CARE AND FITNESS

JO BIRD

INTERPET PUBLISHING

Credits

Published by
Interpet Publishing,
Vincent Lane,
Dorking,
Surrey RH4 3YX,
England

ISBN 978-1-84286-188-2

Editor: Philip de Ste. Croix
Designer: Philip Clucas MCDS
Photographer: Neil Sutherland
Diagram artwork: Maggie Raynor
Index: Amanda O'Neill
Production management: Consortium, Suffolk
Print production: Sino Publishing House Ltd, Hong Kong

Warning

Riding is a hazardous pastime. Horses are unpredictable, powerful animals and even something as simple as leading a horse in from a field can potentially be dangerous. Never underestimate the situation and think ahead. It is advisable to carry a mobile phone and always wear a hard hat and protective clothing when riding. Seek help if you are unsure about any aspect of horsecare or equitation.

Disclaimer

Jo Bird

Jo Bird has owned horses for most of her life and used to juggle working as a groom in the mornings and going to an office job in the afternoons! She now provides management and nutritional advice to people buying horses and has worked in an advisory capacity helping to develop new products for a leading equestrian product manufacturer. She has owned a variety of horses, from foals to aged veterans and from huge, heavy traditional cobs to fine, fit racehorses. Her natural horsemanship philosophy is: 'Think about it from the horse's point of view'. She is the author of *Keeping A Horse The Natural Way* and *Breaking Bad Habits In Horses*.

Acknowledgements

Thanks to everyone at Sworders and to Lucy Back, Michelle Cogger, Ellen Cutlip, Katy Griffiths, Sarah Howe, Jo Jones, Laura Key, Gill Leage, Sarah Pamment, Adele Rawlinson and Gill Walker for allowing photoshoots. Thank you to my brilliant models: Charlotte Ellis, Kate and Lucy Fallen, Harriet de Freitas, Jeanette and Kelly Holzinger, Abbey and Leah Jolliffe, Jeannie Mott, Lotte Notley, Mary-Anne Reilly, Amber Tucker and Alice Watts.

Contents

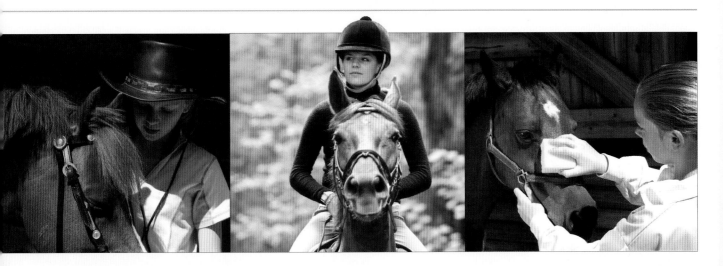

UNDERSTANDING HORSES

How does a horse or pony's mind work? What is important to him? To build a good partnership with a horse it helps to look at things from his point of view and to try to understand what is going on inside his head at any point in the day. Horses do not react to events in the same way as we humans do, and we have to recognise this when we take on the responsibility of looking after a new horse or pony.

COMPANY

Horses are herd animals by nature and therefore feel much more settled when they are in a group. You may have seen how some horses get very distressed if they are left in the field alone, or how some will 'nap' (refuse to go forward when asked to do so) in order to get back to home or to the other horses in a group lesson.

In the wild a herd would be made up of mares, stallions, colts and fillies of different ages, most of whom would be related. Most domestic male horses are castrated (gelded) to enable them to live in the groups we select for them without fighting with the other males or creating unwanted foals by mating with the fillies!

Within the group there is a hierarchy whereby the most dominant horses influence the more subservient ones. This is not always achieved by a display of obvious aggression – you have probably seen horses back away from others who have just swished their tails or flattened their ears in a threatening gesture.

▲ **Take time to understand** how your horse or pony's mind 'ticks'. It will help your friendship to grow stronger.

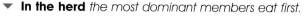

▼ **In the herd** the most dominant members eat first.

◄ **A horse that is relaxed** and contented will often be seen resting with a droopy lower lip like this.

▶ **Horses have very expressive ears** – *we can often learn a lot about their moods by getting to know what the 'language of their ears' means!*

I'm alert and friendly

◀ **The flattened ears and purposeful stride** *say it all – this horse is unhappy with something and is warning others to back off and give him some space.*

I'm relaxed

◀ **Play fighting is usually** *an expression of high spirits rather than a serious confrontation.*

I'm attentive

i'm angry

I'm afraid

▲ **Horses are herd animals.** *In the wild they live in a group that is led by the most dominant member of the herd.*

I'm in pain or unhappy

Food and safety

In a domestic situation horses rely on humans to provide food and shelter. In the wild they cover many miles each day grazing on the different types of vegetation that they come across and seeking out rivers or watering holes from which to drink. The most dominant horses will get to food or water first. In a domestic situation you may see some horses getting bad-tempered if others come too close when they are feeding.

In bad weather, with or without the protection of rugs, horses tend to huddle in a line and 'put their bums to the wind' as – once they get cold or wet – they have to use more energy simply in order to keep warm. Eating plenty of forage, such as hay, actually generates heat within their bodies; however, if food is scarce they risk losing weight in cold temperatures.

Even when a herd of horses sleep, some may sleep standing up (their legs can lock which allows them to sleep standing upright without toppling over). Or several may lie down leaving at least one horse in the group standing 'on watch' alert to any sign of danger.

What is important to us?

What generally makes people happy is seeing a smartly turned out, **clean** horse in shining tack and/or wearing the latest brightly coloured rug.

What is important to a horse?

Good companionship, adequate food and water and the freedom to be able to roll in the dust or mud!

◀ **A particularly pungent odour** *can make a horse curl his lip like this to trap the smell deep in his nasal passages.*

TIP Try not to chop and change grazing companions too often. Feeling part of a familiar herd will make your horse feel settled and content.

◀ **Horses get a lot of water** *from moisture in growing plants, but in hot weather they will not want to stray too far from their water source.*

▶ **Freedom to exercise** *without any constraints will enhance a horse's well-being and fitness. Let him have fun!*

▼ **We like to see a nice clean horse** *but horses* **love** *to roll in dirt. It makes them feel good and helps to relieve an itch or get rid of shedding hair.*

▼ **This pony has lost** *his feed to a dominant companion. Feed times may need supervision so he does not miss out.*

Freedom & Play 10%
Safety 30%
Company 30%
Food & Water 30%

◀ **A Horse's Needs**
Understanding the basic things that are important to a horse will help us to make better sense of its actions when we take on the role of carer.

▶ **Locking Mechanism**
Horses have the ability to lock the joints and ligaments in their elbows and stifles (the hindleg 'knees') to enable them to sleep standing upright without falling over.

Getting to know your pony

Ears Excellent hearing ability, far superior to our own. Each ear can move independently enabling them to concentrate both on close sounds while still being aware of danger by detecting more distant signals. Horses sometimes bolt or spook at a noise that may be undetectable to us.

Eyes His eyes are set on the side of his head. This gives horses almost 360° all-round vision, the only blind spots being directly behind them and below the muzzle. While this is an excellent feature to detect the approach of any predators, unfortunately it also means it is hard to creep up on horse in a field to slip on a headcollar without also being detected! They have good night vision but their colour spectrum is limited – this is not a problem in the wild but it can cause confusion with depth of field when approaching coloured poles in the showring.

Muzzle The hairs on the muzzle are used as feelers to sense objects as horses cannot actually see this area. For this reason, it is best to leave these untrimmed on horses that live outside for most of the time. Their sense of smell is highly acute and they can pick up the smells carried on the wind of other horses or by sniffing droppings left behind. They often display the Flehmen response to a strong or unusual fragrance. This is when a horse raises his head to a horizontal position and curls back his top lip which allows a special organ at the top of the nasal passage to assess an unfamiliar smell.

A relaxed horse or pony will have 'soft' ears, muzzle and nostrils.

Teeth A horse is equipped with large strong incisors to crop off grass and wide molars for grinding his food. The teeth grow continuously and need attention from a vet or equine dentist annually as uneven wear can cause sharp edges and hooks.

The big cheek teeth are the molars which grind up the horse's food.

TIP Get the vet to check your horse's teeth if he will not accept the bit or he drops his food. It is possible sores in his mouth could be a problem.

Skin/Hair A horse's coat grows thick in winter while it sheds hair in summer. It is made up of hair follicles that stand up to trap air to keep the horse warm or flatten to dissipate heat when it needs to cool down. The skin has very acute tactile (or touch) sensation and a twitch mechanism that means the horse can move a small area of skin to dislodge a fly without the need to scratch it.

Tail The tail is immensely adept at swishing away flies and other irritants and it also displays the mood of the horse by the way it is carried (e.g. high and taut = excited, low and loose = relaxed, taut and swishing = angry).

Legs The conformation of the legs (the way that they are formed and shaped) differs widely between different breeds of horse. Some have long, athletic limbs with springy pasterns to cover the ground at speed while others have thicker boned legs with upright pasterns for a short choppy stride, or a straight shoulder and a higher knee action as in a driving horse.

Stomach For such a large animal, the stomach of a horse is really very small – roughly the size of a rugby ball and making up only 10 per cent of the overall volume of the gut. Horses are designed for trickle-feeding, which means that they like to eat little and often throughout the day, such as when they are grazing, rather than having a few big 'meals' like we do.

Hooves The hooves have an outer layer of hard horn (a bit like the nails on our fingers) surrounding the sensitive layers of hoof wall which actually bear the horse's weight. A shock-absorbing sole surrounds the frog – the rubbery V-shaped piece in the centre of the foot – which helps with absorbing the shock of the impact as the foot hits the ground.

WHAT A HORSE NEEDS

SUITABLE GRAZING

The most natural way for a horse to live is outdoors, where it is able to forage and roam freely in a herd environment. Although it is not always possible to offer total freedom outdoors all day long, it is essential for both their mental and physical well-being that horses have access to grazing (or at least a turnout area with hay supplied) for a good portion of the day. Grass is nature's 'super food' but horses also eat herbs, tree leaves and bark for added vitamins and minerals.

- The grazing should ideally be able to supply much of the feed content that the horse or pony requires. For this reason it should not be over-grazed by too many animals – ideally allow 6000sq m (1.5 acres) per animal.
- It needs to be well maintained (harrowed, rolled, topped, rested) and free of weeds.
  - The fields should be well drained so that they do not become boggy in winter.
  - Fencing should be safe and secure.

Remove: Poisonous plants such as ragwort, yew, laurel, privet, rhododendron, horsetail and foxgloves – they can **KILL** a horse or pony.

Control: Weeds such as docks, nettles and thistles. These do no harm to the pony and certainly nettles and thistles have some beneficial feed value, but do not let them encroach into your grass crop and take up valuable room that should be occupied by the grass.

Keep compost separate: Grass cuttings ferment when left in a pile and can cause colic in horses and ponies if eaten. **Never** put cut flowers anywhere where horses might reach them as many are poisonous to them.

▲ **Tailor your grazing** to the needs of the types of horse that are on the land. Grass and herbage are the most natural diet for all equines.

▶ **Know your plants.** These are all poisonous to horses and should be eradicated from any areas that your horse may be able to reach.

Oak

Stable-kept horse

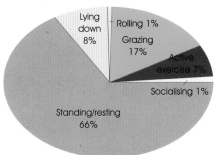

- Lying down 8%
- Rolling 1%
- Grazing 17%
- Active exercise 7%
- Socialising 1%
- Standing/resting 66%

Wild/naturally-kept horse

- Standing/resting 17%
- Rolling 1%
- Lying down 3%
- Socialising 8%
- Grazing 67%
- Active exercise 4%

◀ **Eating wood and soil** may be symptoms of a mineral deficiency so offer a mineral block or a comprehensive vitamin supplement.

▲ **Types of Horse-keeping** These diagrams illustrate just how unnatural modern horse-keeping methods can be. We expect to have athletic animals – yet horses stabled overnight can be almost immobile for around two-thirds of the day, instead of keeping active if they were grazing outdoors.

▲ **A stabled horse will relish** a treat of fresh grass and wild-picked herbs as a welcome change from his usual dry diet of hay and concentrates.

Fern

Ragwort

Rhododendron

Yew

Ivy

Suitable shelter

Shelter is needed in a field so that horses can escape torment from flies and the hot sun, as well as to protect them in wet and windy weather. In the wild horses would walk to find shelter behind a large tree or hedgerow and you should either provide the same natural features or a man-made shelter or stable for any horses or ponies that you are caring for. This should be sited facing away from prevailing winds. If a shelter or barn is to be shared by several horses or ponies, make sure any open sides are wide enough to accommodate several horses at once. This allows them to leave the shelter easily and can prevent accidents caused by squabbling.

WATER

The water content of grass can be as high as 80 per cent but, as it varies tremendously according to the season, horses must always have access to clean water to satisfy their thirsts. Haylage (semi-wilted grass) contains between 35-50 per cent water which is significantly higher than hay which is very dry and which has on average only 15 per cent. This explains why some horses prefer it soaked or they may even dip each mouthful in their water bucket themselves! It can be very dangerous if horses lack water and become dehydrated, and hard work or hot weather will mean that their water intake will increase. A hard-working horse or pony can lose up to 20 litres (4.5 gallons) of sweat in a day. An average of 25-70 litres (5.5-15 gallons) of water derived both from fluid and food will be needed per day. This water is needed to help food pass through the gut and a thirsty horse will stop eating after a while.

Water can be supplied by mains water piped to a trough (or an automatic waterer) or by filling buckets by hand with a hose. A rainwater butt situated next to a field shelter is also a useful way to collect water in a remote place.

Weight 500kg (1100lb)

Water content 350lit (77gal)

▲ **Allow your horse access** to fresh water at all times. In hot weather his water intake will be greater than normal.

◀ **Seventy per cent** of a horse's weight is made up of water. Make sure he gets plenty!

TIP A shelter is the ultimate in horse heaven – he can choose for himself whether to be 'in' or 'out' and is never unnecessarily confined.

▲ **Shelter from the sun** *is as important to horses as shelter from wind and rain.*

◀ **Often horses can sense** *a storm approaching and will get spooked. Make sure they have a shelter available.*

▶ **Site a field shelter** *so that the back bears the brunt of any bad weather. Allow room for the horses to be able to walk around it.*

Suitable stables

Whether you keep a horse at home or on livery, it is likely that you will need some kind of stabling even if he is kept out at grass for most of the time. Stabling offers the horse protection from extreme weather and a safe place to rest or recover from illness or injury. It also means that an owner can monitor the horse's food intake while he is living in the stable area and is easier to watch.

TRADITIONAL STABLES

Traditional stables are smart and safe. Internally they should be at least 3.6m x 3.6m (12ft x 12ft) in area to give the horse or pony plenty of space in which to move and lie down. A courtyard design gives the occupants shelter from the elements plus

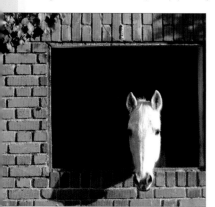

◀ **A window on the world.** *Horses appreciate being able to see what is going on in the environment all around their stable.*

a good view of the other horses. It is becoming increasingly popular to add windows to the back walls too, to give the horse another view to enjoy and to improve air flow through the building.

INTERNAL BARN STABLING

A light airy barn is divided up with rows of stables on each wall and a central corridor. Usually the ceilings are high which helps to maintain a pleasant temperature in both summer and winter. Often internal stabling has grilles between the stables which allow the horses still to sniff and touch their friends even when they are confined.

CORRALS

A concrete or sand/dirt area can be fenced off to confine your horse safely, while still allowing him some freedom and access to the outdoors when he chooses. There should be some shelter provided even if it is just a tarpaulin or roofed area he can walk underneath to avoid the full heat of the sun or a sudden downpour of rain.

Remember: A horse would naturally walk 16-32km (10-20 miles) a day in the wild so being confined to a stable is a very unnatural experience. Even stabling a horse overnight usually means that it will be stuck in the stable for about 15 hours at a stretch. *Make sure that your horse or pony has time in the field or corral every day* in addition to any ridden work that you do.

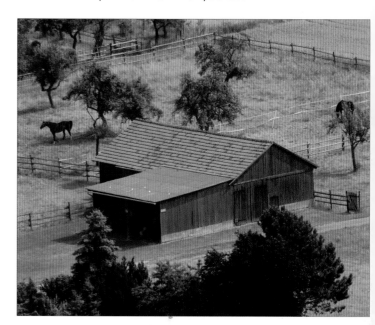

▲ **Stables that lead directly** *to turnout areas are very beneficial to your horse, particularly if he is able to move freely between the stable yard and the paddock.*

Security light

Exterior switches for lighting with waterproof cover

Opening skylight

Good ventilation

Security light

Good drainage

▶ **Stables should be palaces, not prisons!** *This design combines features that will keep a horse or pony comfortable, safe and secure.*

Muck heap

Lockable tack and feed room, with door wide enough for wheelbarrow

▼ **Metal grilles between stables** *allow horses to maintain contact with neighbours.*

Rainwater butt

Concrete base with good drainage

Water tap and hose

Fire extinguisher

Stable cat for rodent control and company

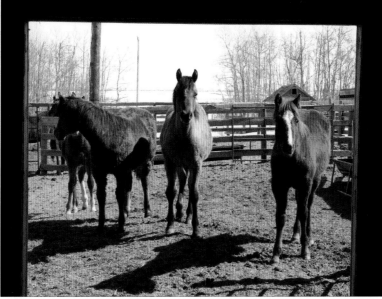

Open window (at rear) to allow horse to put his head out

◀ **This is an ideal set-up** *because the horses can leave the stables and enjoy the company of their stablemates in the fresh air outside when they choose to do so.*

17

Supervision and safety

SECURITY AGAINST THEFT

Horses and ponies are valuable animals and it is unfortunately necessary to protect the animals we love from unscrupulous people who may want to steal them and sell them on to others. Horse equipment, such as tack, rugs, horse lorries and trailers, are also at risk of theft so to avoid the heartache of ponies or property being stolen, do follow the suggestions listed below:

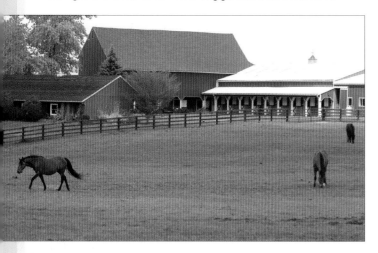

- Keep all entrance gates to yards and fields closed and padlocked at all times.
- Have horses freeze-marked and/or microchipped and display a notice stating that this has been done to act as a deterrent to any would-be horse rustlers.
- Visit the yard/field at different times of the day, so that there are not long, regular periods of inactivity that a thief could take advantage of.
- Mark rugs in paint with your postcode/zip code or the horse's freeze mark.
- If you are not yet old enough to drive, suggest to your parents or the grown-up who helps you to look after the horse that you should paint your postcode/zip code in large letters on the side and

roof of your trailer/lorry so that it can easily be identified by a police car or helicopter if it is stolen. Or recommend that you have a tracking device fitted.
- Have your tack security marked (often the local police will provide this service for you) and make sure all valuable items are insured.

SENSIBLE PRECAUTIONS

Keep a notice on the yard that lists up-to-date telephone numbers of police, fire and ambulance services plus those of vets, farriers and local friends who can help out in an emergency.

Once a week take a walk around all the fields and check the fencing for gaps or breakages and pick up any litter (e.g. bottles, bags etc.) that may have been dumped or blown onto the land.

Check all woodwork in the stable yard for loose nails or splinters (*right*) – these could injure a horse badly. Check metalwork, such as door cappings, hay racks and hinges. Bent or rusty metal can have sharp edges and catch on rugs or injure your horse.

If you are short of time, try to come to an arrangement with other people that they will check your horse for you. A rug that has come unfastened and slipped down, or a sudden bout of colic, could have disastrous consequences if not discovered quickly. Never assume that you do not need to check him every day – horses are very accident-prone!

TIP A combination lock is useful as vets, farriers and friends can be told the code – you won't need to get lots of separate keys cut.

◀ **Sagging barbed wire** can cause catastrophic injuries to horses.

◀◀ **Solid post and rail** provides smart, safe fencing but check for splits in the wood or splinters.

▼ **Walk around the paddocks** weekly and check for hazards, such as rabbit holes and rubbish.

◀ **Security and supervision** are important day and night. Check locks before leaving.

◀◀ **Having your horse freeze-marked** is a good deterrent against theft.

Rugs and blankets

Although a horse is very well equipped to cope with most weather conditions as its coat can shed or lie flat to keep cool in hot weather and grow dense and fluff out to trap a warming layer of air in the winter, there are still times when using a rug or blanket will help to keep him in top condition.

DO use a rug if
- Your horse is obviously cold or shivering.
- Your horse is outside during prolonged wet periods (to prevent a chill or rain scald).
- If your horse is underweight (to help him utilise the food he eats for weight gain and physical energy rather than just to keep warm).
- If the air temperature is cold and a stabled horse will be standing still for long periods or in a draughty or windy environment.
- Even in hot weather a horse may need a thin rug to protect him from midge bites or to keep his coat cool and avoid bleaching from the sun.

DO NOT use a rug
- If your horse or pony is too fat – let him use some of his feed intake to produce body heat naturally.
- If you are unable to check him regularly. With a rug on he is unable to regulate his temperature. The weather can change suddenly and it is up to you to add or remove rugs to keep him comfortable.
- If the rug does not fit properly. Poorly fitting rugs can slip backwards and chafe the horse's skin and loose straps can catch on objects or get caught up in a horse's legs as it moves or struggles to get up.

▶ **A lightweight mesh fly rug** *will stop irritation from biting midges and also helps to prevent sweet itch.*

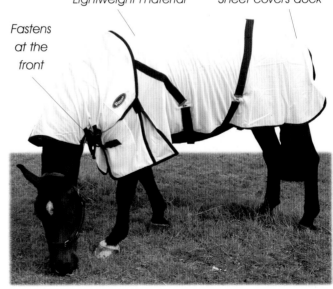

Lightweight material   Sheet covers dock

Fastens at the front

TIP When fastening chest straps, bear in mind that the horse will want to put his head down to eat, so you may need to loosen the higher strap to stop it digging in.

Points of a rug

1 Correct size of neck aperture to fit.

2 Shoulder pleats here on an outdoor rug would allow freer movement.

3 Long enough to cover from top of withers to dock.

4 Darts and shaping along back to improve fit.

5 Breathable material to wick away moisture.

6 Better without a seam on the back where damp can seep through.

7 Tail guards reduce

▲ **Be ready for all weathers.** *Your kit should comprise both light and heavyweight turnout rugs and at least one stable rug (shown above).*

draughts and rubbing.

8 Leg straps reduce slippage but can rub.

9 Deep enough to stop draughts and cover the horse when lying down.

10 Adjustable, secure fastenings.

How to put on a rug

PUTTING ON A RUG

1. Fold the back and front halves of the rug inwards until you are left with a panel not much wider than a saddlecloth. It will be easier to carry and lift over the horse and less likely to flap about and startle him.

2. Unfurl the front section ensuring that the hair remains flat underneath. Fasten the chest buckles first and allow plenty of room for when your pony puts his head down to graze.

3. Work backwards and open out the rug carefully.

4. Pull the tail through the tail loop. Fasten any leg straps. They should loop through each other to avoid chafing and be positioned so they do not catch when the horse lies down.

5. Fasten the belly straps in a diagonal pattern – left strap across to right buckle, right strap into left buckle. Allow a slack of about a palm's width under the belly.

6. A well-fitting rug should not rub or slip backwards.

Well-fitting rug

Rug rubbing on withers

Leg straps too loose

Rug too large

◀ **It is not only the length** *and depth of rug that is important. For a good fit the neck aperture needs to be right or it will rub bare patches on the shoulders or slip back and rub the withers.*

TIP If you have a dark-coloured horse, a white cotton summer sheet can be useful to reflect the sun. This limits bleaching of the coat and keeps him cooler.

TO REMOVE A RUG

Undo the straps from back to front – first leg straps, then belly straps and finally the chest straps (**1**). This is just in case the horse should get loose while you are removing the rug – if the chest straps were undone first, the rug might slip back and get tangled around his hind legs with catastrophic consequences.

Either fold the rug inwards to make it easier to lift off or grasp it at the withers and rump and slide it off backwards (**2**) so that the straps do not knock against the horse.

Your horse's MOT !

In addition to daily care and attention a responsible horse owner will keep up to date with the following matters and items:

PASSPORT

When you purchase a horse it may come with a passport (this is mandatory in the UK). This can be issued by a breed society with details of the specific breeding and exact date of birth if known, or be more general with just a description of the horse's identification markings which have been endorsed by a vet. These include colour, position of whirls (where the hair swirls against the lie of the coat) and any freeze mark, brand or identification chip the horse may have.

VACCINATIONS

These are usually recorded on the horse's passport and it is often a requirement to show proof of up-to-date vaccinations when travelling abroad or competing. Protection against equine influenza (flu) and tetanus are usually essential, while vaccination against equine herpes is a requirement in some racing and stud yards with additional protection being needed if a horse or pony is travelling abroad.

DE-WORMING

Most animals naturally carry some form of internal parasites from time to time, but a heavy worm burden can have serious health consequences for a horse or pony, including weight loss, anaemia and colic. Good pasture management by clearing droppings and field rotation helps with assistance from a carefully planned use of chemical de-wormer, chosen according to the season and specific worm eggs and larvae you are treating. A small sample of manure can be sent to a laboratory to assess if there is a parasite problem.

INSURANCE

Nowadays in our 'sue everyone' culture it is essential to have proper insurance. There are various levels but cover should include at minimum third party claims (for example if your horse kicks another and injures it or damages property like a stable or trailer) and also vet's fees caused by illness or injury. A long-term illness or fracture of a bone or an attack of colic that requires an operation could easily run up fees of several thousand pounds. Without adequate insurance cover it may not be financially possible to save the animal.

TIP Ask your vet to send you a reminder when your horse is due for his annual vaccinations or dental check so you do not forget.

DENTAL CARE

Having good teeth is an essential part of survival for a horse and problems like jaw abscesses, missing or sharp teeth will severely affect their ability to chew fibrous forage and grains resulting in possible impaction colic (a digestive problem where food stops moving along the animal's bowel) or poor nutrient absorption. A dental check by a vet or equine dentist once or twice a year will eliminate discomfort caused by sharp hooks or infected teeth. Horses are usually better patients than we are in the dentist's chair!

and simply have them trimmed and shaped by a farrier every couple of months. Many horses and ponies can be worked very successfully in this way. If you wish to try your horse unshod when he has previously worn shoes, bear in mind the transition will take at least three months and in this time he will have very sensitive feet before they harden up – ouch!

If you will be riding on very abrasive ground or predominantly on roads, then shoeing may be more appropriate. Shoes can be fitted (with the addition of road nails or studs if required) and this will prevent the hooves wearing too quickly resulting in sore or bruised feet. Bear in mind that you will be tied to a six- to eight-week cycle of farrier visits to trim off the excess hoof which is still growing above the shoe. Overgrown feet can put strain on the joints and raised clenches (nails) can cause splits in the hoof wall. If your horse loses a shoe as a result, it means you won't be able to ride!

HOOF CARE

Horses hooves grow approximately 1cm (⅜in) per month and in the wild these would wear down naturally as they roamed around the rough ground of their pastures. It is quite possible to keep your horse's hooves naturally bare

▲ **Farriers have good knowledge** *of anatomy and will help keep your horse sound – whether shod or unshod.*

▲ **Remedial shoeing** *can help with faults – this eggbar shoe can help support a collapsed heel or navicular bone.*

REGULAR ROUTINES

DAILY CHECKLIST FOR A FIELD-KEPT HORSE OR PONY

- **Visit your horse at least twice a day** – it would be dreadful to find your horse caught up in his rug or having been injured and to know that he may have been in distress for a long time before his plight was discovered.

- Take time to check if the horse is grazing calmly or standing looking anxious or uncomfortable. If he is rolling and sweating or rolling incessantly (*above*) he may be suffering from abdominal pain cause by colic. If he is standing awkwardly and is reluctant to move, he could have succumbed to an inflammation of the tissues of the hoof called laminitis (see pages 88-89 for more details).

SUMMER

- Approach the horse and run your hand over his body to check for bumps, bites or scratches that you may not notice from a distance. It is a good idea to feel for excessive heat in the hooves and pick out his feet to remove stones that could cause bruising.

- Some horses wear mesh rugs in the summer to protect from midges biting them or a light-coloured rug to stop the sun overheating them and bleaching the coat.
- Apply fly repellent/fly fringe if necessary.
- Top up the water or tip out and refill the trough or container if it is green with algae or contaminated with food or bird droppings. Stale water is not palatable.
- Pick up the droppings in the field unless you have a large field that can be chain-harrowed by a tractor.

Droppings can be removed either by hand or nowadays large yards often have 'vacuum'-type towable collectors to make cleaning the fields easier. Fields can be harrowed provided they can be rested afterwards and this needs to be done in hot weather to kill off any worm larvae in the droppings.

If your horse or pony is putting on weight he may need to have his grazing restricted by moving him to a corral or stable for part of each day/night.

TRY THIS: On a hot day feel the contrast in temperature of a grey horse compared to a dark bay or black horse.

Or on a coloured or paint horse feel the temperature difference of the dark and light patches!

◀ **In summer it is essential** *to protect pink muzzles with sunscreen or they will blister. Apply daily as it rubs off easily.*

TIP Try to ride when it is cool enough to be comfortable. If he is sweaty afterwards, sponge down the neck, chest, saddle and inner thigh areas and dry him off with a towel.

▼ **This mesh fly mask** *totally prevents flies from irritating a horse's eyes and ears.*

▲ **A fly fringe** *works like an extension of your horse's forelock to help flick the flies away.*

◀ **Raking up droppings daily** *will keep the pasture fresh and reduce the likelihood of flies and worms affecting your horse or pony.*

◀◀ **Provide more than enough water** *to last until your next visit to the field.*

Daily routines

WINTER

- Feel if he is warm enough and put a rug on him if he is losing condition through just trying to stay warm. Put on a dry rug if the one he is wearing is soaked through.
- Feed hay or haylage if the grass is poor and supplement his diet with cereals (see pages 56-57) if he is working hard or requires more condition.
- It is a good idea to add tepid water to any feed – some horses resist drinking icy water and may suffer impacted colic if the feed is dry.
- Break any ice which has formed on the water trough.
- Check the fencing as it can be damaged by high winds or falling branches.
- Even if you are not riding him, examine him thoroughly (although do not groom him too regularly – he needs the natural grease in his coat to stay warm in the cold weather).

- Hose off mud on legs and pick out feet every couple of days (*above*). You may not otherwise see if he is suffering from mud fever or thrush (see pages 88-91) if he is coated in mud.

Note: Horses and ponies can survive very cold temperatures but have more trouble coping with long periods of rain. They can catch a chill and become very miserable and being wet can cause 'rain scald' which makes their hair scabby and fall out in clumps! *Keep him warm and dry.*

EXAMPLE OF A DAILY ROUTINE FOR A STABLED/PART-STABLED PONY

- Morning feed (possibly prepared the night before).
- Depending on the season, change the rug.
- Examine the horse, check for filled (puffy) legs.
- Groom and ride or:
  Put on a headcollar and lead out to the turnout area or pasture.
- Muck out the stable and lay ready for the evening.
- Empty, clean and re-fill water buckets.
- Fill up haynets and hang up ready for the evening (or soak for 10 minutes then leave out to drain).
- Allowing your pony as much time out as possible, finally fetch him in from the field.
- Tie him up outside and pick out his feet.
- Remove any outdoor rug and check over for wounds; brush and re-rug if necessary
- Put your pony to bed in his stable.
- Prepare the feeds for the next day.

Remember: Ponies do not sleep for eight hours or so during the night as we do. They take short naps of just 5-10 minutes (or longer if they choose to lie down) throughout the whole 24-hour period of a day. This stems from their inborn instinct to be ready to flee from danger at any time. You can understand how some horses can get bored when they are stuck in a confined space for long periods.

TIP Use big-bale haylage and water troughs for field-kept horses. This means they can self-feed and will not go short if, for some reason, you are late.

◀ **Horses are very good** at keeping warm even in the snow. Wet weather is more of a problem to them.

You can get a good idea if your horse is warm by feeling the temperature around the base of its ear or behind its elbow.

▲ **Even with a rug** on, you can feel these areas. A sweaty or shivery horse will not be comfortable.

◀ **After hosing,** dry his legs with a towel before turning out or stabling.

◀◀ **Nights are long** for a stabled horse – top up hay as late as you possibly can.

Grooming

FULL GROOMING

If you watch horses reacting to one another in the field, you'll notice that they groom their friends by nibbling with their teeth. So when you give your horse a thorough grooming session you will make him adore you! Imagine the itchiness of the coat they must feel when it is shedding in clumps or the irritation they feel when being bitten by midges – wouldn't it be such a relief to have your entire body brushed if you were in their position?

1. Tie up your horse or pony and remove any rugs.
2. Start at the neck area and using a body brush (or dandy brush if the coat is very long) use long, firm, sweeping strokes following the lie of the coat. Regularly remove hair from the brush with a curry comb.
3. Use a rubber curry comb in a circular motion to remove clods of mud or matted hair. Only use a body brush on the face and legs as these bony areas are very sensitive and can be easily bruised.
4. Using separate damp sponges wipe around 1) the eyes, 2) the nostrils and muzzle, 3) the teat area in a mare and the sheath area of a gelding and 4) under the dock.
5. For the mane, first mist it with some de-tangling spray, comb it all onto the wrong side, then brush it back over in small sections to remove any knots in the hair (inset). If you find that there are stray hairs that insist on sticking up, either dampen them or use human hair gel to set them in place!
6. For the tail, coat it with de-tangling spray and, working on a small section at a time, tease out the knots with your fingers so that the brush will pass through the tail hairs easily. You may have to hold the hairs across your knee to be able to brush the ends of them effectively.

7. Scrape off any mud from the outside of the hooves and pick out the inside of the hoof. Using a water brush dipped in water, scrub off any mud residue from the outside of the hooves.
8. Dip a small towel or flannel in clean water and then wring it out to be almost dry, and then wipe it over the horse's entire body – this will lift the dust (inset detail) and lay the hair flat.
9. Finish by applying a mist of show sheen spray – remember not to put it on the saddle area or you risk a disaster when your saddle starts slipping! After the hooves have dried, a coat of hoof oil provides the finishing touch.

Colour code your sponges *for different purposes or mark them with a permanent pen so you always use the same one on the same area of the body.*

TIP Keep a pack of babywipes (fragrance-free) in your grooming kit. They are a handy way to clean eyes, nose and dock instead of using damp sponges.

If your horse has not had a thorough makeover for a while, his tail may have grown overly long. Trim it square at the bottom roughly 10cm (4in) below the level of the hock. Show sheen applied to the tail every time you groom will help prevent the hair from breaking and knotting. If you horse has long feathers on his legs, apply the spray here too and work it through with your fingers to repel water and mud. Chalk powder or whitener sprays can be used to neutralise staining and brighten white hairs.

Grooming

A QUICK GROOM

If you have limited time before riding, or your horse is living out in the field and excessive grooming is not advisable (you do not want to strip the oils from his coat), then a quick check over and groom is sufficient. He may not look gleaming but he should be comfortable enough to be ridden.

1. Tie up your horse or pony and remove any rugs.
2. Concentrate on the areas where the tack will go as mud here would chafe and make him sore. Remove any dried mud from the head with a soft brush or your fingers. If the mud is wet, use a damp sponge and then dry the area with a towel.
3. Brush away any mud from the saddle area and particularly the area under his tummy where the girth will lie, just behind the elbow.
4. Pick out his feet.

PROTECTION AIDS

On a day to day basis it is unlikely that your pony will need to wear any boots or bandages but for more demanding outings, such as jumping or cross-country events where he may be likely to take a knock or his legs will come under additional strain, then they can be a useful addition to your basic tack.

When you first pick them up, often it is hard to work out whether a boot is for the foreleg or the hindleg. Usually boots designed to go on the hind legs will be longer and may have more fixing straps. The straps should always be fastened on the outside of the leg, with the ends facing backwards.

Did you know?

- Over-reaching is when a pony's hindlegs travel too far forwards and catch the heel of the foreleg, sometimes causing a cut.

▲ **Your horse may want** *to groom you too – it's only natural but sometimes it may hurt – ouch!*

◀ **Poor conformation** *can cause a crooked action like 'brushing' which may result in knocks to the legs.*

Stepping out too far ▶ *with a hindleg can cause an 'over-reach' injury to the foreleg.*

TIP It is faster and safer to use modern boots fixed with velcro straps for ridden use than attempt to bandage legs with cotton or fleece bandages which require special skill to fasten correctly.

▲ **With brushing boots** the strike pad should face the inside. It should be positioned below the knee and just cover the inside of the fetlock.

Wrap the boot tightly round so it will not slip down and fasten the fixings securely, with the straps on the outside and facing backwards.

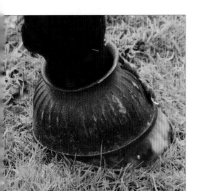

◀ **Over-reach boots protect** *from injury should the horse step on himself with the opposite foreleg or hindleg.*

▶ **The value of protective boots** *can be seen in action as this athletic animal takes a fence.*

Hoof care

Hoof care is vitally important as without healthy hooves your horse or pony may easily go lame. The farrier is as important as a vet as he will examine and rebalance the hooves by trimming and shoeing them correctly, but you need to practise general health care as well. Something as simple as a small crack or a trapped stone could make your pony unridable for several weeks if left to deteriorate. Common problems include bruised soles, cracks and chips in the hoof, abscesses and thrush infections.

1. Tie up your pony with a quick release knot.
2. Fetch a shallow rubber bucket or feed bowl reserved for the job. You will use this to catch the dirt that you clean out of the hoof. This will save you time sweeping up afterwards.
3. Stand parallel to your pony, facing his tail. Bend down or squat so you can easily move away if he should kick out.
4. Run your hand down the back of his leg and lift the hoof from the fetlock. If he resists, lean against the shoulder (foreleg) or quarters (hindleg) of the leg you are cleaning as this will shift his weight away from this leg and make it lighter to lift.
5. Lift his leg up and cup the hoof in the palm of your hand.
6. Tuck the hoof pick into the top corners on either side of the frog (just behind where the shoe finishes). The frog is the 'V'-shaped fleshy part that extends out

from the heel.
7. Using a heel-to-toe motion scrape out the mud, trapped bedding or stones being careful not to prick the sensitive frog.
8. Some hoofpicks have a brush attached which is very useful to clear away fine debris and dust.
9. When the hoof is clean, slowly and gently lower it to the ground and move on to the next hoof.

Warning: Some ponies are reluctant to lift their hindlegs very high as this unbalances them and they may kick out in protest. Be gentle and keep the leg low enough to be comfortable for them. Always be aware when working around the hindquarters of a horse – you can be badly hurt if a horse kicks out suddenly and catches you with its hoof.

There are various hoof products available on the market which do different things. Hoof hardeners will toughen the hoof wall and sole and are useful for barefoot horses or those with hooves that have been weakened by frequent nail holes. Hoof oils serve mainly to enhance the appearance of a healthy hoof. Hoof moisteners assist in nourishing and maintaining moisture within the hoof to try to prevent cracking.

▶ **Learn the points of the hoof** *so that you will understand when your farrier gives you advice.*

White line (junction between horn and sole)

Wall (horn)

Bulb or heel

Bar

Frog

Collateral groove

Point of frog

Sole

▶ **A tiny trapped stone** *can cause bruising which can make your horse lame. Thoroughly pick out each of the hooves getting into all the crevices and corners to remove any grit. Hooves impacted with mud or wet bedding risk contracting thrush (see page 90).*

TIP If you always pick out your pony's hooves in the same order he will probably learn to anticipate you and lift each leg up in turn ready for you – what a star!

▲ **To lift a horse's hoof,** *gently slide your hand down the tendons and lean into the horse to shift his weight over from the leg you want to raise.*

An obstinate horse will lift a hindleg if you squeeze the hock. Lift from the pastern or feathers and support the weight with your hands.

▲ **Hoof hardener** *strengthens the structure of the hoof wall and sole in an unshod horse.*

▶ **Hoof oil** *adds a nice sheen for a smart appearance.*

Bathing

For tip-top presentation for a show or to freshen up a pony in hot weather, a bath can be beneficial. Some shampoos also benefit the horse or pony by helping to repel flies or eliminate scurf too.

Only consider bathing your pony if the weather is warm or he could catch a chill. In colder temperatures treat any dirty areas with a stain-remover spray and just clean stains section by section by dabbing them with a damp sponge.

Some ponies dislike water altogether and some have a fear of hosepipes – the shape may remind them of a snake hiding in the grass perhaps! For nervous ponies and in anything other than the hottest of weather, it is advisable to fill buckets with warm water so as not to alarm the pony and keep him comfortable.

1. It is easier to do one side of the pony in one go and then move round to do the other to avoid him standing with a wet coat for too long a period. Dampen the coat, then massage in the shampoo working it well in with your fingers – your pony will love this!

2. Work the shampoo through the hairs of the mane. Do the same with the tail or lift the bucket up so that the tail dips into it and swill it around to give it a thorough rinse through.

3. With a water-laden sponge or a watering can drench the shampooed coat, working from the back downwards to thoroughly cleanse the coat of the shampoo. A tolerant pony may allow you to use a hose to do this. Repeat until the water runs clear and no traces of soapy foam can be seen.

4. Using a rubber sweat scraper, work from neck to tail with long strokes following the lie of the hair to remove excess water.

5. Stand to the side of the pony and hold the tail hairs just below the dock. Keeping the dock portion still, spin the lower hairs like a windmill to get excess water off the tail – tell everyone else to get out of the way or they are likely to get a soaking!

6. To finish rub him over with a clean towel, paying particular attention to the base of his ears, his elbows and legs and heels. Use a waffle weave cooler or a sweat rug (with a cotton rug on top if the weather is cool) to allow the water to evaporate while avoiding the risk of the pony getting a chill.

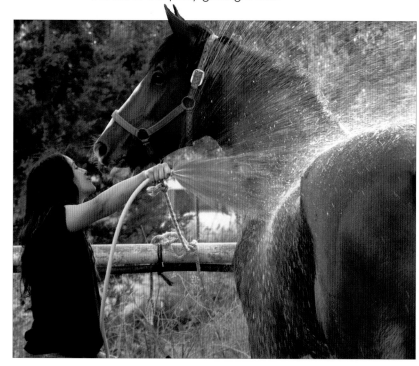

TIP A horse's tail can be washed throughout the year to keep it clean and tangle free. The horse will not feel cold unless you soak the dock – then you will see him shudder!

1 *Dampen the coat, then massage in the shampoo.*

2 *Rub shampoo into the mane and tail hairs too.*

3 *Rinse the coat thoroughly to remove the soap suds.*

4 *Most of the water will be squeezed out with a sweat scraper.*

5 *Towel dry to prevent him from getting a chill.*

6 *Use a waffle weave cooler rug to wick away any moisture.*

Should I clip my horse?

Horses naturally shed their coats in the spring and begin to grow a thick dense coat in the autumn to keep them warm during the winter months. Many horses can manage without a rug during the winter provided they can find shelter from prolonged rain.

The downside to having this thick coat is that when we ride or work them actively, they will soon get too warm and start to sweat. This sweat is uncomfortable for them and it will make their coat sticky and difficult to groom, even when dry. If you only ride your horse a couple of times a week, then it is probably better to put up with this than risk him getting cold or having to wear several rugs because you have clipped him. If you ride your horse regularly and the sweating is becoming a problem, then consider clipping him.

But which clip should you choose? Ideally only take off the minimum of hair in the areas where he sweats – usually the neck and girth area. Remember that your horse will have to wear a rug if you take off some of his coat unless the weather is very mild. A clip will usually last for about six weeks before it needs to be re-done.

SUMMER CLIPPING

It is not usual to clip when spring is approaching as this may affect the summer coat that is coming through. Some horses do not lose their coats readily or they naturally have thick coats all-year-round and in such cases it is kinder for them to be clipped during the summer to keep them more comfortable.

HOGGING MANES

Some horses have their manes cut off (hogging). You will see polo ponies with hogged manes and also some heavy cob types. If a pony has sweet itch, it may be smarter and kinder to hog his mane rather than leave him to rub it until it ends up looking like a loo brush!

▲ **Neck and Chest Clip**
Useful for horses living out that sweat when ridden as most of the coat remains.

▲ **Trace Clip**
Ideal for working horses as it keeps them cool and makes grooming easier.

Warning: Do not hog a horse on a whim! It takes nearly a year for the mane to grow back fully and in the stages in between your pony's hair will stand up vertically like a 'mohican' haircut!

CLIPPING FEATHERS

Some native and heavy breeds grow long hairs around the coronet and pastern and these feathers (as they are called) can stretch up as high as the back of the knee. Although stunning to look at, they need a lot of care and attention and can soak up wet and mud like a sponge which makes them very heavy and difficult to dry out. You may want to cut off the feathers to prevent mites burrowing in the long hairs or simply to change your horse's appearance – from hairy heels to short and smart! So perfect your clipping skills!

Warning: Clipping involves sharp, fast-moving blades and often electrical equipment. It should only be done by experienced people who can handle the horse and the equipment safely.

TIP Ask a helper to stretch out each foreleg while you clip the elbows to avoid nicks to wrinkly skin.

▲ **Chaser Clip**
Similar to the Trace Clip, but all or part of the head hair is clipped too.

▲ **Irish Clip or Low Trace**
Ideal for most working horses as only areas that sweat are clipped of hair.

▲ **Blanket Clip**
Useful for working horses and smart for those with hogged manes.

▲ **Hunter Clip**
For stabled and hardworking horses. Leg hair is often left on for protection.

◀ **Some people choose to** *remove whiskers from the muzzle. Horses use these as 'feelers' so it is kinder to keep these if possible.*

▶ **Keep the mane tied** *out of reach of the clippers and remember that you cannot put back what's clipped off!*

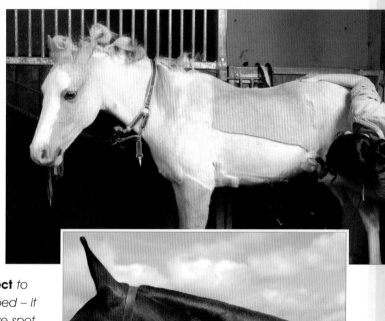

◀ **Many horses object** *to having their ears clipped – it may tickle in a sensitive spot or sound like a buzzing fly!*

▶ **On the right type of horse** *a newly hogged mane looks absolutely superb.*

Mucking out

The repetitive daily chore of cleaning the stable can be a bug-bear to many horse owners. If you do not have the benefit of extensive grazing or are tied by rules of a livery establishment, it is likely you will have to stable your pony for part of the day and/or night. In that case you will be faced with the fact that you will have to muck out the stable on a regular basis.

From the horse's point of view, bedding has the following functions: it
- provides somewhere comfortable for them to lie down, preventing possible knocks and injury.
- allows them to stale without splashing their legs.
- provides insulation and a non-draughty environment.
- enables them to dig around in the bedding material and carry out foraging activities which a bare concrete floor would not allow.

TYPES OF BEDDING

Straw

A straw bed can look wonderfully inviting – even soft enough for us to sleep on! Wheat straw is cheap and readily available while barley straw makes the softest, golden-coloured bed. The straw you use should be dry, non-dusty and mould-free. Although it makes the cosiest of beds, unfortunately straw is probably the hardest type of bedding to muck out and it creates the biggest muck heap!

Note: Many horses will eat a straw bed and while normally it should do them no harm, a greedy pony could suffer colic or put on undesired extra weight by excessive consumption of straw.

Chopped Straw

As it sounds, this is composed of short strands of straw, supplied in plastic wrapped bales so they can be stored outside. Clean and easily biodegradable without creating a vast muck heap, they are an excellent choice for all but the wettest of horses.

Shavings

Wood shavings supplied in a plastic wrapped bales give the cleanest appearance and tend to be the most absorbent type of bedding. They are more expensive and the bales are heavy to handle.

Hempcore

Stems of the hemp plant are supplied in plastic-wrapped bales. It offers high absorbency in a shallower bed but can be harder to manage than shavings and is an unappealing dull grey/brown colour.

TIP Take your pony out of the stable before mucking out, as disturbing the bed will cause dust particles to be released into the air that will not be good for his breathing.

▶ **Many horses learn to regard** *their stable as a place of safety where they can rest. It is our responsibility to provide a comfortable dry bed with forage to help them relax while they are confined in a stable.*

Check that any bedding you buy is free of mould and dust.

▲ **There are many types of bedding** *on the market so it is important that you should weigh up the pros and cons of each in relation to your budget and your horse's needs.*

Shredded Paper

Recycled paper put to good use. In fact it is quite possible to shred your own newspaper but you will need a mountain of papers and a production line of people to produce enough for a bed!

Rubber Matting

Compressed rubber sheets (*right*) which have excellent insulation and shock-absorbing properties. They can be used on their own or covered with a thin layer of bedding which is banked up at the sides. After the initial cost outlay rubber mats make a huge difference in terms of speed and ease of mucking out.

How to muck out

The tools you will need are:
- A wheelbarrow.
- A shovel.
- A fork (wide-pronged for dealing with straw and narrow-pronged for shavings).
- A stiff broom.

1. Remove all feed and water buckets. You do not want them contaminated with dust and dirt when you are shaking and moving the bedding around.

2. Begin by lifting any obvious piles of droppings with your fork or shovel. Tip them into the barrow while trying to leave behind as much of the bedding as possible. Throw the clean bedding high onto the banks.

3. Pick up the droppings that are then exposed – use gloves to protect your hands and keep them clean if it is too fiddly working with a fork.

4. Using the shovel, dig out the areas of wet bedding.

5. Sweep the centre of the floor clean and, if you have time, leave it to dry out.

6. Fork down the clean bedding that you had thrown up to the sides and lay the floor of the bed. Unless you are using rubber mats, this should be around 15 to 30cm (6 to 12in) deep (depending on the type of bedding used) so the floor will not be exposed by the feet of the pony when he moves or lies down.

7. Add some fresh bedding on top if the bed is now getting thin.

8. Rebuild the banks to protect the pony from draughts and keep him away from the walls – otherwise you risk him getting 'cast' (stuck) when he tries to get up. Finally, with the back of the fork, flatten the bed and shape the banks. What a smart bed!

DEEP LITTER

A deep litter bed means that just the droppings and the worst of the wet bedding are removed without disturbing the main body of the bed. Fresh bedding is just added on top so that it is dry for the horse to lie down on. This is useful if the horse is kept in a barn as the whole barn can just be dug out periodically by tractor.

Advantages:
- It takes a lot less time on a daily basis.
- A full muck out is only required every month or couple of months.
- It uses less bedding and so is more economical.

Disadvantages:
- When the bed is eventually dug out, the bedding is **so** heavy and it **really** smells.
- The air in the stable can become stale or smell unpleasantly of ammonia.
- If the bedding gets too wet, the horse will lie in this soiled material and he also risks contracting 'thrush'* in his hooves from the wet environment.

*See section on ailments – page 90 – for explanation of thrush.

TIP If you visit your horse late at night to feed him, take the opportunity to skip out any droppings so they won't get mixed into the bed overnight.

SKIPPING OUT

This term is used when you just remove the surface droppings that have been left since the bed was last properly mucked out. Use a shovel or fork to gather them up or do what many people prefer to do and put on rubber washing-up gloves and scoop them into a bucket or basket known as a 'skip'.

▲ **For a quick clean-up,** *use rubber gloves and simply pick the droppings up off the surface.*

▲ **For a more thorough clean,** *a barrow and fork are needed to cope with all that wet muck!*

Cleaning tack

Apart from mucking out, one of the hardest jobs in horse care is cleaning tack. Tack soon gets greasy from the horse's sweat and, if left in this way, it can rub causing sores on the skin. The leather itself will also suffer and may crack or go stiff or develop mildew if left damp. Cleaning tack need not be a chore; it can be very rewarding – the end result is clean, shiny tack and, of course, your pony will look so smart!

CLEANING YOUR SADDLE

1. Put your saddle on a saddle horse, or the arm of a chair, fence rail or stable door.
2. Fill a bucket half-full of warm water and add just a drop of detergent as this will help to dissolve any grease.
3. Remove the girth, stirrup leathers and irons from the saddle.
4. Take the irons off the leathers and drop the irons in the bucket of water to soak.
5. Dip a sponge in the water and squeeze it out so it is damp (but not saturated) and wipe over the entire saddle, lifting up the saddle and girth flaps and not forgetting the underside.
6. Pay attention to greasy areas. Small spots of grease are referred to as 'jockeys' and you may need to use your finger nail or a teaspoon to scrape them off. (Do not use a knife or you may scratch the leather.)
7. Now either apply liquid soap onto the tack or rub the tub or bar of saddle soap with your damp sponge and apply it to the leather.
8. You will notice how the leather shines after the soap is applied.
9. Clean and soap the stirrup leathers and re-fit the irons. The finished job looks great (**10**)!

Girths made of material or webbing should have the hair and mud brushed off and be washed in the washing machine. You can pop a sock over the buckles at each end of the girth or wash the girth inside a pillow case to protect the machine.

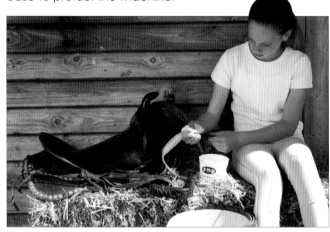

▲ **Cleaning tack** *doesn't have to be a chore. It is good to know your tack is safe, well cared for and gleaming!*

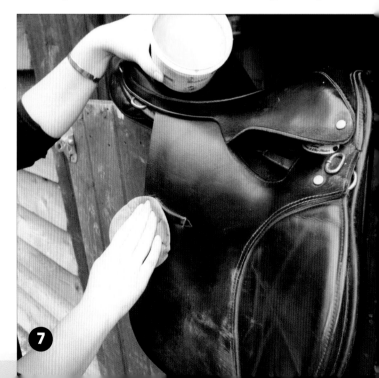

7

TIP If you want the leather to look shiny, keep your sponge as dry as possible when applying the soap to prevent it going frothy and streaky. Think of it as a polish, rather than as a soap!

Cleaning your bridle

1. Find somewhere to hang your bridle – a coat hook will do.
2. Either take the bridle to pieces (warning: you must know how to put it back together again!) or take all the straps out of their keepers but keep the buckles done up.
3. Begin on one side and work your way down from the headpiece to the bit, wiping over the leather with a sponge dipped in the water and detergent.
4. When you reach each buckle, make a note of what hole it is on, unfasten and wipe over it, and then immediately re-buckle it (**5**). Work your way down the other side removing any grease and mud. Clean the reins thoroughly too.
6. Wipe over the bit with the wet sponge. If it is soiled with dried-on dirt you may have to soak the bit in warm water to loosen this (**7**).
8. Apply saddle soap, unfastening and refastening the buckles and billets as you go along. Try not to get too much soap near any stitching as these are best left as dry as possible.

Note: Never be tempted to use household soap as saddle soap is a **very** different product. Not only does it clean the leather, but it also contains glycerine and waxes to feed, protect and waterproof the leather. Saddle soap comes in different forms: spray, creamy liquid, soap bars and in tubs.

Synthetic saddles do not need soaping ever – simply brush off the hairs and wipe over them with a sponge dipped in water and a drop of detergent.

▲ **Your tack is the link** *between you and your horse. You don't want brittle or greasy leather chafing his skin.*

TIP If you do a lot of competing, it may be helpful to have a 'rough' bridle and a 'show' bridle that is only kept for best.

1

3

6

7

8

Turning out

It pays to stay safe when leading your horse out. A horse that barges into you or drags you will soon learn that he can get away. Good manners are essential!

1. When entering the stable push your pony's chest and say 'back' to move him away from the door.
2. Slip on the halter or headcollar but again make sure he stays back and does not crush you against the door in his eagerness to get out.
3. Open the door wide and go out just ahead of him.
4. Keep just in front of his shoulder when leading him. It is traditional to walk on the left of the horse.
5. When entering the field walk through the gate and then turn the horse to face it as you close it (below).
6. Remove the headcollar with the horse still facing the closed gate before saying 'Off you go' or something similar so he knows that he is free to go.

Never release a horse which is facing into the field – he may bolt off to see his friends with you still holding the rope.

CATCHING YOUR PONY

Some ponies are little devils at being caught! If you are rushing to get your horse in to saddle up for a ride, or because bad weather suddenly sweeps in, it can be infuriating having to walk 17 laps of the paddock in an attempt to catch him! You need to have some tricks up your sleeve to gain the upper hand.

DO

- Spend time in the field with your horse and use it to bond with him by giving him a titbit, or a rub, or some personal attention while you are picking up droppings.
- Catch him simply as a reason to do 'nice' things. Take him out of the field for a feed (a couple of carrots perhaps) and then return him to the field without working him.
- If you know he is bad to catch, fence off the field into several small paddocks so that he can't get too far away from you.
- Keep your body language friendly –

◀ **Do not let your horse barge** *out of the stable. Say 'back' and move him away from the door.*

TIP Offering a horse a titbit as you are about to release him is a good way to make him stand calmly and not attempt to bolt off in a cloud of dust!

approach him from the side heading towards his shoulder, rather than head-on, and keep your eyes and arms lowered.

- Give him a treat as a reward once you have the headcollar on him.
- Persist in catching him. If he comes to realise that you will give up quickly, he is more likely to be awkward. If he knows you will keep going until you do catch him, he may feel that he would rather not exhaust himself!

DON'T

- Allow anyone to aggravate or tease horses in the field or they will steer clear of anyone who is approaching them.
- Enter a field with a feed bowl unless there is only one horse in it, otherwise you will be mobbed and could be trampled. Keep any treats hidden in your pocket.
- Just catch your horse in order to ride him. He may

start to dread you coming if he is always taken away from the field to work.

- Leave a headcollar on the horse in the field unless it is made of leather which will break under pressure, or is a specially designed safety headcollar. An unbreakable halter could get caught up on an object and lead to the horse injuring himself quite badly.
- Don't flap the headcollar or march up to the horse aggressively.
- Don't smack or shout at the horse once you do catch him – even if it has taken you an hour and you are furious!

▲ **You will rarely tire** *a pony by chasing after him to catch him – you will be the one who ends up worn out!*

◀◀ **Approach from the side** *and walk towards his shoulder with eyes and arms lowered.*

◀ **Fencing off the field** *into several smaller paddocks will stop him from running too far away.*

FEEDING AND NUTRITION

All ponies should be treated as individuals when it comes to feeding because, as with people, their age, build, and breeding or 'type', as well as the workload they are being asked to do, have a huge bearing on dietary needs.

- Some ponies can almost live on fresh air – these are termed **good doers** or easy keepers.
- Others can be fed large volumes of highly nutritious feeds but still look like a bag of bones – these are known as **poor doers**.

Although it is not a hard and fast rule, good doers tend to have more laid-back characters whereas poor doers can often be worriers or have sharper, more edgy personalities.

Assessing condition If you run your hand over the side of a horse or pony it should feel smooth but you should still be able to feel some of his ribs, just below the surface of the skin. A thin horse will have prominent ribs, a bony rump and a 'tucked up' appearance. An overweight horse may have pads of fat along the crest of his neck and over his shoulder (just in front of where the knee rolls are on the saddle). He is also likely to have a huge backside!

You may think that your horse lacks energy and so increase the quantity of feed you give him in the hope that it will pep up activity levels. However, this is not the case as both an underweight and an overweight pony may appear lethargic. Balanced nutrition is needed to add condition slowly and to bring an underweight horse back into shape. Simply increasing rations will not speed up an overweight pony – he needs to shed weight and build muscle tone through increased exercise to become more forward-going.

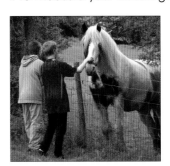

Remember: A weigh tape is a useful tool to keep an eye on changes in weight so why not see just how heavy your pony really is! You use it to measure your horse's girth and then read off the probable weight from the scale that is printed on the tape.

◀ **Visit your horse daily** *and supplement his grass with feed if necessary.*

Very poor condition

Poor condition

Moderate condition

TIP Horses prefer several smaller meals to one huge blow-out. By using carrots and short chops, you will keep him chewing for longer.

▼ **A weigh tape is useful** to calculate your pony's approximate weight.

Position it across the base of the withers and around close to the elbow.

▲ **A quick glance isn't enough.** *Learn to see and feel weight change that may happen gradually. Feel for the ribs and for pads of fat being laid down.*

▲ **Nutrition is an art** *which needs careful balancing according to your horse's condition and workload. You will probably have to make changes throughout the year.*

Too far back (like this) will give a false reading.

Good condition

Fat condition

Very fat condition

Components of the diet

Fibre: Keeps the 'engine' of the gut functioning properly. Found in: All forage – grass, hay, haylage, chaffs.

Protein: The building blocks of the body's cells. Protein is needed for a pony to grow, to build muscle and repair damaged tissues after strain or injury.
Found in: Many grains and fresh grass.

Carbohydrates: These are organic compounds that occur in food, such as sugars, starch and cellulose. Roughly 75 per cent of all plant material is a type of carbohydrate and so is the primary source of energy for a horse.
Found in: Grains and fresh grass.

Fats: These provide a lot of calories for energy. If they are not used up through physical activity, they can be laid down as fat in the body and cause weight gain. Found in: Oil is present in cereals or can be added to the diet in liquid form (*below*).

Vitamins and minerals: These are organic compounds that are vital for the overall good condition of the body. They also are present in green plants and cereals. They help to keep horses healthy.

Forage: This should be the mainstay of the diet. This may be grass, haylage, hay, short or long chop (e.g. alfalfa or straw chaff).

Remember: If you are changing the type of food that you feed your pony, such as switching from pony nuts to a higher energy mix, make the change gradually. It takes time for the bacteria in your pony's gut that aid the process of digestion to adjust to breaking down different foods. Begin by replacing part of the old food with a handful of new food and then build up to the new diet over a period of three or four days.

▼ **Forage should ALWAYS** *be the mainstay of the diet. From grass to dried alfalfa, forage comes in many forms.*

TIP If you have a rodent problem, choose pelleted feeds instead of grains, as these are very digestible to your horse but not as tasty to rodents!

◀ **Horses will naturally** browse at herbs, bushes and trees if they are given the opportunity.

▼ **As hay will make up** the bulk of your horse's ration, inspect it carefully before purchase.

Straw-based chaff

Mixed food

◀ **There are endless brands** of short chops, mixes and pelleted feeds on the market. Every bag of feed will list the contents analysis and should suggest the type of animal to which it is best suited.

▲ **A selection of chaffs** plus carrots can make an interesting high-fibre feed without grains.

Pony nuts

Alfalfa chaff

Preparing and giving feed

A horse should eat between 2 per cent and 4 per cent of his overall bodyweight each day – depending on breed, type and workload. Therefore an average 500kg (1100lb) horse may require approximately 12.5kg (27.5lb) of food per day.

Weight guideline
SMALL BALE OF HAY between 25-35kg (55-77lb)
ROUND SCOOP OF CHAFF Approx 300g (10oz)
ROUND SCOOP OF OATS/CUBES Approx 2kg (4.4lb)

When calculating how much to feed:
- Be aware that the percentage figure includes all the grass/hay that he will consume in addition to any concentrates.
- Remember that a scoop of chaff weighs much less than a similar scoop of mix, so weigh out the feed until you are familiar with the amounts – guesswork won't do!

Use a weigh tape to assess your horse or pony's overall bodyweight and re-measure him every month to monitor weight fluctuations. Observe him when he eats for signs of quidding (dropping excessive amounts of food from the mouth, usually a sign of a dental problem). Take notice of his droppings – if they are excessively runny or have whole grains or long fibres still present in them, this may be a sign of poor digestion. Maintain a good worming routine or your horse will not enjoy the full benefit of the expensive food you are giving him and could suffer permanent gut damage.

HAY

Do choose good quality hay – it should smell fresh and not be too brittle or dusty. Know the source of your hay so that you can be confident that it does not contain dangerous weeds.

Do not use hay which is overly dusty, smells stale or has areas of mould as this could lead to breathing problems.

Do store hay in a dry, airy space. Keep it covered to prevent contamination from birds, rodents or cats.

Do feed hay loose on the floor or in a haynet or low-mounted trough. A high-set hay rack is not ideal as this feeding position is unnatural – horses naturally eat with their heads lowered. Also dust can more easily be breathed in or get in the horses' eyes causing various health problems.

Do soak hay if it is at all dusty – but only for five to ten minutes. Longer soaking would remove some of the precious nutrients.

Advice on how to tie up a haynet can be found on pages 60-61.

▶ **A typical diet** *may comprise mix or cubes and/or short chop.*
1. Measure or weigh out the feed into the bowl.
2. Add any supplements/ herbs or tonics if required.
3. Just before feeding dampen with water to help digestion (do not add water too early unless you want to soften the feed as cubes will begin to disintegrate).
4. Finally stir the mix well.

TIP Keep feeding simple. Manufacturers do the hard work and design specific diets for different horses so you don't have to worry!

▲ **If hay needs soaking** to make it less dusty, submerge it for around five minutes. You may need to put a weight on it to stop it floating up .

▶ **Hay should be fed** off the ground or at a low level to limit dust inhalation.

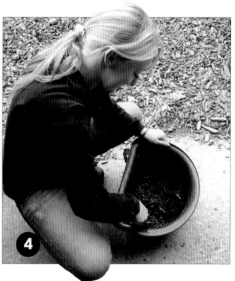

Short chops and concentrates

Short chops are fibrous foods like straw and alfalfa which have been machine-cut into short lengths. They are used to bulk out short feeds (rations fed from bucket or manger given in addition to forage) or as a hay replacer fed from a bucket or manger. Concentrates (or hard feed) are foodstuffs that are low in fibre but high in other nutrients. Grains and grain by-products, pony nuts and cereals are typical examples. Listed below are some guidelines on how best to use them.

Do use a wall-mounted feed manger or a flexible trug which will not cause injury if left in the stable.

Do not use a standard 'builder's bucket' (*right*) as the horse could get its headcollar caught up in the handle or be injured should the plastic split.

Do store feed in rodent-proof storage bins or dustbins. Sweep up any spillage so as not to attract vermin.

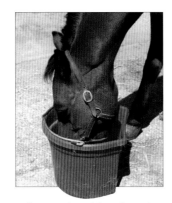

Do check the 'Use by' dates on the sacks of feed and use them in rotation. Discard any feed that is out of date or that has got damp.

Do divide the day's ration into several small 'meals'. Horses are trickle feeders and are designed to feed little and often to gain the most benefit from their food.

Do make changes to the diet gradually over a period of three to four days by replacing a proportion of the old ration with the new feed and gradually building it up to the full volume of the new feed ration.

Do have a noticeboard visible where you can write down your horse's feeding routine for others to follow in your absence.

Remember: If you are feeding a lot of chaff, it is beneficial to moisten the feed slightly with a little water to make it less dusty and easier for the horse to swallow. A watering can gives you greater control than splashing water in from a bucket.

YUM!

Succulents like carrots and apples are a real favourite, especially when grazing is limited. Carrots are full of fibre so can be fed in high volume without producing a lively horse – a bucket full of carrots will keep a horse satisfied without making him fat or fizzy. Keep them whole so he has to spend time chewing them up or, if you must cut them, **only** slice them lengthways, **never** in rings as these can get stuck in the throat.

KEEP FEEDING SIMPLE

A commercial pre-prepared feed should not need to be supplemented with vitamins if it is fed at the recommended levels (guidelines are usually on the sacks). You do not need shelves full of supplements, herbs and tonics – they only complicate matters!

A mineral or salt lick should be available at all times in the pasture or stable.

FEEDING IN A FIELD

When feeding horses at pasture, tie them up individually to the fence if they are likely to squabble. Place feed bowls at least two horses' lengths apart and watch them at all times. Horses are notoriously greedy and aggressive when feeding, so keep at a safe distance and carry a schooling whip if necessary to make them back off if you need to.

TIP Damp feed soon goes stale and mouldy. Storing your feed in feed bins will keep it dry, fresh and safe from rodents.

▼ **After tipping the feed** *into bins, label the lid of each bin with its contents to avoid guesswork!*

▲ **A rubber feed trug** *is safest as it won't split if the horse tramples on it.*

◄ **Competing may** *mean a long day out so take your horse's feed with you.*

◄◄ **When feeding in a field,** *spread feeds widely apart so horses will not squabble or miss out.*

Feeding guidelines

Pleasure Horse (Light Work)

This is a horse or pony ridden about three times a week and rarely pushed to exert himself for any long periods. Most of his 'fuel' should come from grazing or forage with any vitamin or mineral shortfalls being supplemented.

Daily ration: 2-2.5 per cent of bodyweight

80% Forage
- Grass/hay

20% Concentrates
- Maintenance mix
- High-fibre cubes

Dietary Extras • Succulents
- Fresh (or dried) herbs

- Turn out as much as possible
- Hawthorn, rosebay willowherb, rose hips

Games Pony/4-H Pony/Showjumping Pony/Show Pony

An active pony but one which may only be required to work hard at weekends, having several days off work each week which may predispose him to weight gain. A higher energy mix could be used on the days when he is working hard, reverting back to high-fibre cubes on rest days.

Daily ration: 2-2.5 per cent of bodyweight

70% Forage
- Grass/hay

30% Concentrates
- Maintenance mix
- High-fibre cubes

Dietary Extras • Succulents
- Fresh (or dried) herbs

- Turn out as much as possible, in yard if necessary
- Hawthorn, garlic, cleavers and meadowsweet are useful herbs

Feeding a **Poor Doer** or **Fizzy Type**

Often of Thoroughbred ancestry, these types may cause a problem as forage alone does not provide the calorie intake they require to maintain a good weight, but too much energy will make their already exuberant character unmanageable. Turning them out for as long as possible will help them to relax and allow them to expend some energy. The slightest distraction or a stressful situation will hamper their nutrient absorption still further. Yeast or probiotics added to the diet will assist in optimum gut function.

TIP Leave a mineral lick out for a 'good doer' on a forage diet to ensure he gets the full spectrum of vitamins – but check it does not get devoured in just one day!

Daily ration: 2.5-3 per cent of bodyweight

70% Forage
• Grass/hay

30% Concentrates
• Conditioning mix
• Alfalfa/lucerne
• Probiotics   • Oil

Dietary Extras • Succulents
• Fresh (or dried) herbs

• Turn out as much as possible
• Valerian, hawthorn, chamomile and meadowsweet are useful herbs

Event Horse (Hard Work)

These horses work consistently hard across a wide spectrum of activities requiring precision as well as power. They may find it hard to switch off and recharge their batteries and so it is essential to assist their mental and physical well-being to achieve optimum results.

Daily ration: 2.5 per cent of bodyweight

65% Forage
• Grass/hay

35% Concentrates
• Working/ competition mix
• Alfalfa/lucerne
• Vitamin/mineral supplement
• Probiotics   • Oil

Dietary Extras • Succulents
• Fresh (or dried) herbs

• Turn out as much as possible
• Electrolytes may be needed occasionally
• Ginkgo biloba, watercress, dandelions, beech and hazel branches enhance the diet
• Whole corn cobs (maize) provide energy as well as stimulation while being eaten

Veteran Over 20 Years (Retired or Semi-retired)

Older animals often have a decreased ability to absorb nutrients effectively. They often lose condition and may have problems chewing due to worn or loose teeth. Despite their light workload they need higher sources of energy/calories and also good available protein and calcium. If they have trouble eating hay or grass, high-fibre cubes can be fed with sugar beet pulp to provide fibre.

Daily ration: 2-2.5 per cent of bodyweight

70% Forage
• Grass/hay

30% Concentrates
• Veteran/conditioning mix
• High-fibre cubes
• Alfalfa
• Oil
• Sugar beet pulp
• Probiotics/yeast

Dietary Extras • Succulents
• Fresh (or dried) herbs

• High calcium, high protein
• Turn out as much as possible
• Cider vinegar is a useful addition to the diet
• Willow, meadowsweet and comfrey are useful herbs for animals with arthritis

Haynets

Even if you feed hay from the floor or a manger there are times when you will need to use a haynet, perhaps when your pony has to wait outside for the farrier for a long time or to keep him occupied when travelling in a lorry or trailer. Tying a haynet safely is a very important thing to learn.

1. Fill the haynet and gather up the cord to close it.
2. Thread the end of the cord through the tie-ring in the stable/trailer and pull the haynet up until the centre of it is level with the pony's chest.
3. Thread the cord through the net as low down as possible as this will help to stabilise the net as it gets emptied by the pony eating the contents.
4. Bring the cord back up towards the tie ring and tie it in a quick release knot (as shown below right). The weight of the net will keep it taut but you will still be able to release it quickly and easily, if you need to.
5. Finally, turn the whole haynet around so that the knot is at the back of the net.

Too high – the pony is straining unnaturally to reach the hay and seeds and dust could fall in his eyes.
Too low – the net flaps around and the pony could get caught up in it.

Ultra-Quick Release Knot
1. Thread the cords through the tie ring, then the net, and pull up to the required height.
2. Make a loop and hold it with your left hand.
3. With your right hand pass the free end behind the hanging cord and then forwards through the loop, making a second loop.
4. Release the first loop with your second hand and pull down on the second loop. This will make the knot tight.

The free end can be threaded through this loop for extra security.

If you need to soak your hay, a haynet will make life so much easier. Use a large container filled with water and submerge the haynet for up to ten minutes to minimise the danger of dust and spores being carried out of the hay by draughts of wind. Hang the haynet up on the yard fence to drain – this will make it much lighter to carry and stop the stable bedding getting wet or your legs getting soaked as you carry it to the place where you are going to secure it!

▲ **A haynet may look** *full but it is the weight of food that you supply, not the volume, that is important.*

▲ **Tie the net high** *but below horse's eye level. Use a quick release knot so it is easy to refill.*

TIP Buy several haynets so you can fill several days' worth in advance to save precious time.

◀ **Soak hay only** *on the day it is being used as damp hay can soon turn mouldy. Submerge for five to ten minutes (no longer or the nutrients will seep out). Hang up to drain* **outside** *the stable for a few minutes or you will soak the bedding. Change the soaking water every couple of days.*

▲ **Even if you normally feed** *from the ground, a haynet is useful when you are travelling or when your horse is tied up waiting for some time.*

PROBLEMS – WE HAVE THE ANSWERS

I DON'T HAVE TIME TO RIDE

This is a common problem and it can be frustrating and weigh on your conscience knowing you are not giving your pony enough exercise. It only takes a few weeks for a pony to become unfit and put on weight if he is out at grass. If he is stabled, confinement for long periods of time can lead to stress and depression starting to reveal itself in the form of stable vices (such as crib-biting, wind-sucking and box-walking) and even aggressive behaviour.

Even if you have limited time, you can give your pony some valuable physical exercise by lungeing or loose schooling him (see below for explanations of these terms). You will save time because:

•   The horse or pony does not need to be wearing any tack (other than a halter for loose schooling or a lungeing cavesson headcollar), therefore you save time in getting ready.

•   As you are not riding and full riding attire is not required (except for a hard hat in case you are knocked over and gloves for holding the lungeing rope), you should not get sweaty or dirty, so you can go straight out afterwards without needing to wash or change.

Even spending as short a time as ten minutes a day either lungeing or loose schooling your pony will almost certainly reap great benefits.

Loose schooling requires a round pen, corral or arena. You don't even need to spend time fitting a lunge line. It is quite possible to sit in the middle of the corral simply shouting 'Trot on' and flicking a whip occasionally. The horse gets exercised and you can read or do some homework while he is working.

IF YOU HAVEN'T TIME TO RIDE – FIND A SHARER FOR YOUR PONY

For the average owner it is often very hard to find enough hours in the day to keep a horse or pony well exercised, mentally stimulated and properly fed and cared for in addition to all the chores owning a horse entails. A good solution is to find a sharer. He or she can lavish care and attention on your pony when you are not around and your pony will benefit from the extra exercise and fuss that he will receive from an additional person. They may even help out with the boring chores too!

It is important to choose any sharer carefully and be certain that they are responsible and sufficiently capable of looking after or caring for your pony, or that they will have any necessary assistance or be supervised by a responsible adult. You may find your pony improves in both temperament and performance if, say, he has the benefit of exercising with two riders – for instance, one who is prepared to put in the time schooling and improving his jumping ability, and another who simply enjoys a quiet hack out (this is the pony's 'chill out' time).

▲ **Stable vices are often caused** *by lack of mental or physical stimulation.*

▲ **Poor management** *of this horse has caused him to be depressed.*

◀ **Lungeing is a** *type of exercise in which a horse is attached to a long rope and moves around the handler in a circular path.*

▼ **There is no line** *in loose schooling but often a round pen is used to keep the horse contained while he exercises.*

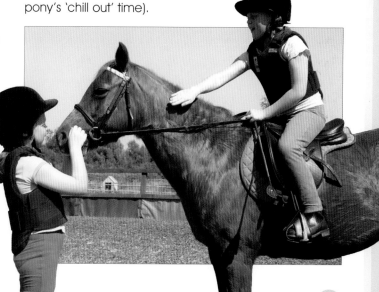

I don't have time to ride

Lungeing can be done in any type of arena or in an open field. The horse wears a 'lungeing cavesson' (a padded headcollar with three swivelling rings on the front of noseband). A long rope called a 'lunge line' (usually about 10.5m/35ft long) is clipped to a ring on the noseband to link the horse to the handler.

1. The only equipment you need is a hard hat and, most essentially, gloves. Without gloves you can get nasty rope burns if the horse pulls against you and causes the rope to run swiftly through your hands.
2. Adjust the lungeing cavesson so it fits snugly around the pony's head. If it is loose it will rub as the pony moves and may even slip across over his eyes which would make the pony very sore.
3. Attach the lunge line to the centre ring on the noseband. (You could use the side ring nearest to you but then you must remember to change it to the other side if you change the direction in which the horse is travelling).
4. Take the loose end of the lunge line in your left hand, bend your arm up and collect up the slack in the rope with your right hand, wrapping it over your left arm – from hand to elbow, to hand to elbow – until it is at a manageable length.
5. Face your pony sideways in the direction you want him to go. As you face him you should hold the slack of the rope in your hand nearest his head and the lunge whip in the hand nearest his tail.
6. Keep the whip low and move it slowly to encourage him to move off. There is no need to 'crack' it sharply or your pony may jump out of the arena in surprise!
7. Release the slack until the pony is moving out on a circle large enough for the pace he is doing (about 6m/20ft for trotting and 9m/30ft for cantering).
8. Use voice commands delivered in a high pitch to

A

B

quicken up the pace – 'T-ROT ON' – and in a low pitch to slow him down – 'W-H-O-A'.

9. Ensure you exercise him evenly on both reins working around the circle in both directions.

A. *Keep your body facing your horse's belly and the whip pointed at his tail when requesting forwards movement and maintain this arc.*

B. *To slow him, angle yourself in front of the movement, facing his head. Pointing the whip at his shoulder will prevent him turning in.*

▼ **Moving your position** *further behind him will encourage him forwards if he is lazy.*

On chilly dark nights when riding time is limited, a 15-minute lungeing session will get the blood pumping and keep you and your horse warm!

◀ **Check the cavesson** fits snugly so it will not move during exercise and rub. The line is attached to one of the rings on the front of the pony's nose. Coil the excess rope up so it does not tangle.

▼ **Use voice commands** – horses learn very quickly and it is rewarding to get a reaction without using the whip.

My pony has scared me – I don't want to

The pattern of horse ownership rarely runs smoothly. Horses and riders both have 'off days' but you must not let a bad experience put you off.

Everybody falls off! Your pony may shy at a bird in a bush, put in an evil buck before a canter or dump you in front of a show jump. It really **does** happen to everyone so don't be despondent.

1. Establish some ground rules

- Take charge of your pony on the ground. You need to be the boss (firm but fair, of course) in your relationship.

Goal: Practise some groundwork skills.

- Backing the horse up establishes that he cannot encroach on your personal space.
- Moving his quarters by fingertip pressure on his sides will make him more responsive.

- Practise trotting him up alongside you, halting and then making him back up – you want quick reactions from him.

2. Believe you both can succeed

If you are having problems jumping or lack confidence in your ability as a rider, it helps to assess both your and your pony's abilities separately.

Goal: Gain confidence from good experiences.

- Have a few lessons on several other ponies – then you **know** you can cope in different situations or jump successfully when you need to.
- Get an experienced rider to school or ride out on your pony to address his problems. Watch how your pony behaves and how the rider deals with any hiccups.
- Now that you and your pony have both gained in confidence, skill and experience, you are ready to put the partnership together under the guidance of an instructor.

◀ **Don't let one bad** *experience make you fearful of progressing with your riding skills.*

ride him!

TIP Talk to other riders, read books and have lessons. Even the most confident riders are learning constantly through their experiences.

◀ **Riding should be fun** *not stressful. Ask for help if you are nervous or confused.*

▶ **It may help** *to watch someone else ride your horse and prove to you that he is up to the task.*

◤ **Backing up a horse** *puts* **you** *in the 'alpha' dominant position.*

▼ **Making him yield** *to pressure will help on the ground and in the saddle.*

He won't let me catch him in the field

Never underestimate the intelligence of a horse! They will see you a mile off and if they don't want to be brought in from the field they certainly will give you the run around! Here are some useful Do's and Don't's to help you overcome this problem if you have a horse that loves to give you the runaround.

Don't always just catch your horse to ride him or he may start to resent you, as you interrupt his freedom to make him 'work'.
Do catch him to give him a stroke or a treat or just to say hello.

Don't enter a field full of ponies with a feed bowl or you will be mobbed.
Do carry a treat hidden in a pocket that only your horse will get. He'll learn to look forward to your special attention.

Don't march up to your horse waving your halter – you'll seem threatening to your horse and he may run off.
Do keep your arms low (hiding the halter if necessary) and eyes looking down so you appear submissive.

Don't approach him directly from the front or creep up behind him to surprise him.
Do approach at an angle level with his shoulder so he can see you clearly.

Don't immediately attempt to get the halter over his nose as soon as you reach him.
Do stand at his shoulder, feed the treat with one hand and then slip the rope over his neck with the other.

Don't hurry or your sense of panic may transmit itself to the horse and you may annoy him by being rough.
Do gently pass the halter over his nose and head calmly and quietly.

Do stroke him on the neck and talk nicely to him as you lead him away.

TIP: To overcome the problem of ponies that are terrible to catch, it is important to spend lots of time with them in the field, approaching them regularly and then walking away again so they do not believe they will be caught each time that you approach. A good time is when you are picking up droppings on your grazing. A leather or safety halter can be left on them when they are in the field to give you a further advantage in that you will have something secure to grab onto.

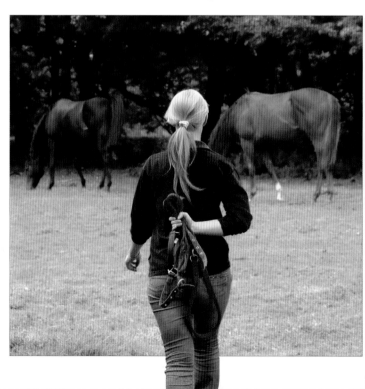

TIP Spend time in the field just 'horse watching'. You will learn how horses interact and they will see you as part of the herd.

◀◀ **Marching head-on** *towards your horse swinging the halter can seem threatening to him.*
◀ **A nervous horse** *is quickly on his toes and faster than you!*

▲ **Approach your horse** *from the side so he can see you and walk slowly with eyes and arms down.*
▼ **Slip the rope** *over his neck and then put on the halter without being rough or in a rush.*

I need to improve my handling skills

Horses are herd animals and, in their natural environment, would soon find their rank in the herd, some being more dominant and some more docile and subservient. As handlers and riders we become part of their herd and so we need to establish our status as their carer and their leader in a sympathetic manner that earns their respect but does not provoke fear.

Problems that can arise from poor handling can include: being dragged or the horse running off when being led, barging out of the stable, acting aggressively when being fed, biting, kicking and general boisterous behaviour. Try to follow these guidelines to avoid problems like these cropping up in your relationship with your horse or pony.

- Always move around horses in a purposeful manner. Horses can easily pick up on any nervousness that is felt by their handlers and this can create skittish behaviour like pulling back when being tied up or fidgeting as you put on a rug, whereas a confident, systematic approach will exude calmness and provide reassurance to the horse.

- Always approach horses in a way that gives them plenty of visual or audible warning that you are coming. If you approach them from behind, say their name or speak some form of greeting so that you do not startle them.

- When dealing with a dominant animal, wear gloves, a hard hat and sturdy boots at all times. Carry a whip to create distance between you should he try to barge or run into you.

- Practise 'backing up' a dominant horse. A dominant horse will chase off or threaten other horses to get them to back away from food etc. and this establishes respect. Gain similar respect by doing likewise – you may have to begin by pushing his chest or tapping a whip on the ground but eventually just saying 'Back' or marching towards your horse with a dominant posture should be enough to get him to move away.

- When you enter the stable, make your horse back away from the door. This will limit his ability either to barge out past you or crush you against the door as you bolt it behind you.

- When you feed your horse in the stable, do not allow him to snatch at the feed as you bring it in. Make him back away and place the bucket down or fill the manger before you allow him to approach it.

- Allow your horse time to see, approach and sniff any new object (like rugs, brushes, feed buckets) that might alarm him if they are suddenly used near him.

- Talk calmly around horses. Stroke and scratch them

TIP Attaching the leadrope to the side ring on the halter will give you more leverage when you are leading a powerful, strong horse.

on the neck, shoulder and withers rather than 'patting' them which is actually nothing less than a little slap!

- Do not regularly feed titbits from your pockets or your horse will expect them and begin to hound you for them (potentially chewing your pockets to get at them). He may well get grumpy if you have forgotten them one day!

LOOK FOR ADVICE

Ask for help if you are having difficulties. A nervous horse being looked after by a nervous inexperienced handler is not a good combination. Understanding horse language comes with experience so never pass up the offer of guidance from an experienced person. It may prevent an accident in the future!

TIP: When leading a strong horse, keep his head close and slightly turned towards you. Do not let him get in front of you. Having his head facing slightly towards you means that his quarters will be angled slightly away from you which will limit any chances of him kicking out at you.

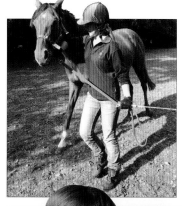

◀ **Bracing your elbow** *into his neck gives more leverage when leading.*

▼ **Barging is bad manners.** *Insist your horse goes back when you enter the stable with his feed.*

◀◀ **Clumsy or boisterous** *horses need teaching that only* **you** *can push* **them** *around! Mimic the action of a dominant horse.*

◀ **Backing up** *a horse keeps him out of your 'space' and asserts your authority.*

GETTING YOUR HORSE FIT

FIT FOR THE SHOWRING

Having a good show horse is not simply a case of arriving at an event with a horse with good conformation that is well groomed – although presentation does plays a big part. A show horse should have good 'core strength' to be able to carry himself well and feel light to ride and very easy to control. A show horse is likely to carry slightly more weight than one used for other more athletic disciplines and have a good 'top line' of muscle tone.

Obedience and suppleness are needed rather than simply stamina so schooling will play a big part in getting your horse in shape for the showring.

- A SHOW HORSE needs exercise for three to five days a week. It should consist of slow controlled work plus relaxed hacking (*above*) so this level of exercise is easily achievable by most riders.
- RIDE LOTS OF TRANSITIONS this will get your horse more responsive and light in the rein contact.
- CIRCLES AND SERPENTINES will improve suppleness and help if you have to do an individual show at a competition.

- WORKING LONG AND LOW will release tension in his back and help create a strong top line rather than a forced outline.
- ALWAYS WARM UP AND COOL DOWN gradually to avoid the risk of muscle strains.
- KEEP HIM ENTERTAINED to prevent him becoming stale by varying your schooling and hacking out regularly to keep him keen.
- FREQUENT GROOMING will dispel the dust and make him gleam as well as creating those 'feel good' benefits of massaging the horse's muscles.

Feeding: A diet made up of 80-95 per cent forage plus a leisure or cool mix concentrate feed is ideal. Adding corn oil will add weight (if needed) and bring a gleam to his coat.

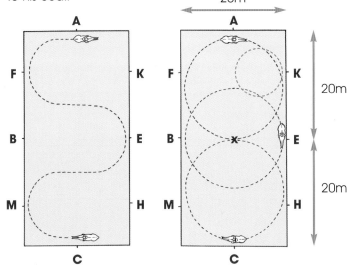

▲ **A serpentine** links semi-circles and changes of direction to keep your horse supple and responsive to your aids.

▲ **Circles can be done** at many points in the arena. Pay attention to making an accurate shape whatever the size.

TIP To avoid spooky behaviour on the day, get your horse accustomed to the sights and sounds of a showring by staging a 'mock' show with your friends.

▶ **Working long and low** *makes the horse stretch and use his top line.*

◀ **Fitting a roller** *and elastic side reins will help build muscle.*

▼ **The side reins** *help the horse step into the contact rather than falling on the forehand.*

Fit for showjumping

A horse predominantly used for showjumping needs to be powerful enough to cope with the exertions asked of him and light enough not to put undue pressure on his joints, ligaments and tendons from the impact of landing after a jump. A showjumper has to put in short bursts of athletic energy – this is very different from the low-impact exercise expected of a show horse or the sustained periods of stamina required by an eventer or endurance horse.

- A SHOWJUMPER needs to be exercised five or six times a week, although it is crucial to examine legs daily for signs of strains/injury which could be worsened by exercise.
- CORE STRENGTH can be achieved through schooling. Practise collection and extension in each pace to improve lightness and responsiveness.
- RAISED POLES AND HILL WORK will increase muscle tone in his hind legs for improved strength of propulsion and power on take off.
- SHORT BURSTS OF CANTER and gallop on a hack will keep him fresh and help him stretch his frame fully.
- JUMPING a variety of uprights and spread fences at home will give you both confidence and help you succeed when in competition.

▲ Loosen up your horse *with massage and stretching exercises before work.*

▼ Vary his workload. *A horse can become stale if his life is purely showjumping.*

Feeding: A diet made up of 70-80 per cent forage plus a working or competition mix is ideal. Alfalfa and sugar beet would be a good base to add to the mix. Remember to cut down on the amount of concentrates that you supply on his days off.

TIP Make short-term goals, as well as long-term goals, and draw up a timetable of when you will ride and the exercises planned for each week.

▲ **Lungeing over poles** *boots the horse's confidence because he can solve striding patterns while unencumbered by a rider.*

◀◀ ◀ **Raised poles** *and asymmetric grids will keep your horse alert and prevent him from rushing.*

SHOW PRESENTATION

It is always encouraging to be told that your pony looks fabulous so let us look at some tricks and skills needed for stylish show presentation to transform a scruffy pony into a competition winner.

1. Bath your pony

- In addition to general dust and grime, ponies which are shedding or changing coats will often look scruffy. By giving them a thorough bath, initially with an antibacterial shampoo and thereafter with a mild equine shampoo, you will enhance the appearance of the coat. Don't forget his mane and tail too! *(See the section on how to bath a pony on pages 36-37.)*

2. Trim up your pony

- A straggly looking tail, unkempt mane and a hairy head will do nothing to give the impression of a quality pony.
- Trim the whiskers and any hairs under the jaw.
- Trim any hairs that protrude from the ears.
- Cutting the hairs away from the heels gives a sharper outline.

Tail: Ask someone to place their arm under the dock of your pony's tail. This will give the approximate height at which it will be carried when your horse is moving actively. Now cut the bottom of the tail so that it finishes 8-10cm (3-4in) below the level of his hock. A nicely squared off tail is known as a 'banged' tail.

3. Plait your pony

- Trim or pull the mane to a length of about 10-13cm (4-5in) long and wash both the mane and tail a couple of days before the show. Newly washed hair is too slippery to plait!
(For instructions on how to plait a mane or tail see pages 78-81).

4. Finishing touches

- Add hoof oil to clean dry hooves to make them shine.
- A little baby oil or highlighter cream on the muzzle and around the eyes will enhance the face.
- Baby oil or detangler spray brushed through the tail will keep it silky and knot-free.
- How about some quarter marks – a chessboard effect or a star or two on his quarters and he will stand out from the crowd.

◀ **Bathing gets rid** of sweat and dust that makes the coat dull.

▶ **By brushing** against the lie of the hair, a stencil can be used to give a stunning effect on the hindquarters.

TIP Often people need help at a show to hold the horse or fetch and carry items. In exchange you could ask for a lesson in show presentation.

◀ **Cut the tail squarely** *across for a neat appearance. Normally 8-10cm (3-4in) below the hock is about the right length but don't be too scissor-happy!*

◀ **Trimming parts** *like the heels and coronet, ears and whiskers give a sharper outline which helps to give your horse a more classy appearance.*

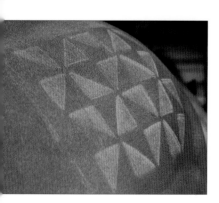

▲ **This horse just exudes** *quality and good health with his gleaming coat and perfect presentation.*

▶ **Bandages look smart** *but may have to be removed before going in the showring.*

How to plait a mane

Does your pony look like he has been dragged through a hedge backwards? Do your plaits look like a row of angry hedgehogs having a fight, rather than elegant braids? Here's how to improve the situation and produce a beautiful plaited mane.

What you will need:
- Elastic plaiting bands (the same colour as the mane)
- Comb
- Hair gel

1. Aim to have an odd number of plaits (11 or 13 is usual) along the pony's offside (right) side of the neck, plus one on the forelock. Divide the mane into equal sections about as wide as the palm of your hand. Put a band loosely round each to keep them separate before you begin to plait.

2. It is normally easier to start up near the ears as it is easier to adjust the lower sections if you have to make any adjustments towards the end of the whole job of plaiting the mane. Take the first section, comb it through and if there are any spiky hairs along the crest, smooth them down with the gel. Divide the section into three equal portions.

3. Begin plaiting by crossing the right and left sections alternately over the middle section. Keep the plait as tight as possible for a tidy effect.

4. Plait as far down as you possibly can, until you only have a few thin hairs remaining.

5. Put a band tightly round the base of the plait and fold the loose ends in before looping the band round again to give a neat end.

6. Fold the plait in half underneath itself so the end faces back to the crest. Secure with a band.

7. Roll or fold the plait back underneath to make a tight ball tucked into the crest of the mane. Smooth down any stray hairs and wrap a final elastic band around it to secure the ball.
   Work your way down the sections, trying to keep each 'ball' the same size and at the same level as the others. As you reach the withers you may have to use a wider section of hair to get the same size 'ball' but be careful that you do not plait too tightly against the neck or it may pull painfully as the pony moves.

TIP It's neater to have too many plaits that look small than too few plaits as large as tennis balls!

▲ ◥ Comb the forelock *forwards and start with a french braid taking sections of hair from each side. Then plait right to the end of the forelock. Roll the plait once for a longer braid or twice for a ball, and secure with a band.*

▼ A horse's neck *can be greatly enhanced by clever plaiting of his mane. Set the plaits high if your horse has an underdeveloped neck or low if he has a thick crest. It really works beautifully as a finishing touch.*

8. If there are a few stray hairs remaining, you may want to trim these off completely to give a sleek line from withers to the first plait.

Finish by plaiting the forelock and rolling it up into a neat ball too. Wow! How smart does he look now?

Caution: Although using a needle and thread to secure the plait in a 'ball' is tidier than a band as the thread is almost invisible, the greatest care must be taken not to prick the pony with the needle or drop it in the bedding where it will almost certainly be lost and cause an injury at a later date.

How to plait a tail

A tidy tail shows off the pony's quarters and finishes a smart turnout. In order to plait a tail the hair must have been left to grow long on the dock, that is it should not have been 'pulled'. Brush the tail through thoroughly before you start.

1. Take two small sections of hair from the very top left and top right of the tail.

2. Cross the right section diagonally over the left section and hold with your left thumb and forefinger. Take another section from the left, just below the first so you now have three strands with which to plait.

3. Take another section from the right, adding it to the first and fold them into the middle. Proceed downwards in this way.

4. Keep taking sections from left and right as you work down the tail, keeping the plait taut.

5. Decide where to finish the French plait, usually at the end of the hairless underneath part of the dock. Continue one long plait with just the hairs you are holding.

6. Put a band on the end to keep the plait in.

7. Fold the end of the single plait back up making a loop and fix with a band.

8. Tuck in any stray hairs or lay them flat with gel. Spray the plait with hairspray to help fix it in place. The tail will fan out better if the bottom is cut square.

Remember: Practice makes perfect so have a go in your spare time!

TIP Hair is easier to plait if it is not too clean and slippery. Wash it a couple of days before the event and do not spray detangler on the dock section!

3

4

▲ **A well plaited tail** *emphasises the muscles of the horse's quarters.*

7

8

▶ **A natural tail** *will protect the pony more and takes very little upkeep as it can purely be plaited on the day of a show. A pulled tail looks tidy but must be regularly thinned or pulled to or it will resemble a loo brush!*

Putting on a tail bandage

Using a tail bandage will:

- Protect the tail from rubbing on the lorry or trailer should your pony be forced to lean back to keep his balance while the vehicle is moving.
- Keep the tail clean.
- Keep the hairs lying flat on a pulled tail and keep a plaited tail secure.

1. Hold the rolled-up bandage in one hand and pass the loose end under the dock and over the top of the tail as high up as possible.
2. Pass the rolled-up end across.
3. Fold the loose end downwards.
4. Then wind the bandage round again to hold the flap in place. Work your way down the tail, winding the bandage diagonally downwards. Overlap the previous layer by half the width of the bandage each time.
5. Keep the bandage totally flat, any creases will dig in and be uncomfortable.
6. When you get to the end of the dock, change direction and go back upwards, aiming to finish half way up.
7. Tie up using the tapes, looping them round and tying on one side of the tail (to avoid a pressure spot if the horse leans on his tail).
8. You may find your pony now has an oddly shaped tail! Don't worry – just gently bend it into its natural curve.

TIP: If your pony has a light-coloured tail, try using a long 'bag' to contain the length of the tail which can be held in place by the bandage overlapping it.

TIP If your pony clamps his tail down try tickling underneath the top of the dock and he should lift it – as if by magic!

Remember: If you have bandaged over a plaited tail, unravel it gently so as not to disturb the hairs. With a natural or pulled tail the best way to remove the bandage is to simply undo the tapes, hold the top of the bandage with both hands and slide it all the way off. Keep your bandage tidy by rolling it up afterwards.

▲ **Undo tapes** *and slide down the bandage.*

Get set to travel

Now your pony is clean and smart, you need to be able to transport him safely to show him off at a competition. Unfortunately many horses and ponies are not keen on being transported due to fear caused by a previous bad experience, or just the feeling of unfamiliarity of leaving companions and the claustrophobic environment inside the horsebox.

The day of the show is not the time to be attempting loading into a lorry or trailer for the first time – so get practising beforehand!

Before the day:

1. If possible leave the lorry or trailer somewhere in the yard where it can become a familiar feature to your horse or pony.
2. Leave the ramp down (a trailer must be attached to a car for it to balance safely) and lead your pony up to it allowing him to sniff it.
3. Move any partitions to make the area seem as large possible.

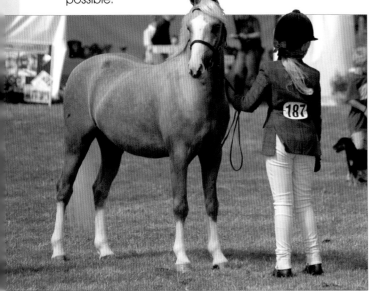

4. By placing a bowl of feed inside you may find his stomach will overrule any feelings of fear and he will march up the ramp willingly!
5. If he hesitates, do not rush him but reward any positive steps he takes with a titbit or a stroke.
6. Ask someone to lead a well-behaved horse into the lorry or trailer first to give him confidence.
7. Once inside, give him some food and just stand there for a few minutes before leading him out again.
8. Practise regularly, feeding and grooming him inside so he is happy to be tied up in the lorry or trailer.
9. Ask someone to put the ramp up while you stay

watching him, ideally with another horse beside him for added reassurance.

10. If possible get him driven around on a short circular journey so he gets used to the motion but soon comes back to the security of his home. **GOAL:** Practise so that your pony walks straight into the trailer first time.

Poll guard

Tail bandage with tail guard

Travel rug

Travel boots   Travel boots

TIP Learn the dress code for your particular class or event – looking good will give you added confidence!

GOING SHOWING – YOUR ACTION PLAN

Everyone is nervous when they first go to compete at a show. Will you remember all your kit? How will your pony behave? How will you feel in the ring? What do you actually do when you turn up to make sure you're entered in the right event? This check list will help to calm your nerves by listing useful tips to help you prepare for the big day.

- Tell you instructor that your aim is to do a ridden show class.
- Watch at a show, or groom for a friend who is competing, so you know the procedure – where to get your number, find the warm-up arena and the judging ring.
- Watch a video on showing and turnout so you can see what the judge will be looking for.
- Design your individual show – keep it short and simple (walk, trot and canter on both reins).
- Practise the halt and salute so your horse knows to stand still.
- Pull or shorten your pony's mane if it is to be plaited – this may take a few sessions.
- Check you have a showing jacket, shirt and tie and smart gloves and boots – you can buy good second-hand gear if you need to keep the costs down.
- Practise bandaging your pony's legs and loading him into a trailer. It is no good you both looking perfect but you can't get to the show!
- Get schedules for local shows – these are often advertised in the local newspaper or schedules are often pinned up in tack/feed shops.
- Ask friends to stand in line with you on their ponies and then watch you practise your individual display so that you won't be so nervous on show day.
- Send off your entry in plenty of time.
- Write a list of all the equipment you will need on the day for you and the pony – clothing, tack, cleaning sprays etc. And don't forget plenty of food and drink and a haynet for your pony!
- Bath the pony a day or two before the show and trim up any hairy bits.
- Plait up on the morning of the show and remove any stains on the coat. Cover him with a light travel rug and put on his boots ready for the journey.
- Off you go and good luck!

TREATING COMMON AILMENTS

'Horse watching' is one of the most informative ways of learning about horses. Watching natural behaviour and being familiar with your pony's appearance and disposition on a daily basis should help to alert you if your horse is under the weather. Any changes to the way he looks or behaves may be indications that there are underlying health problems.

GET TO KNOW THE FACTS

- Find out if possible his past medical history – if he is predisposed to certain ailments (such as laminitis, see page 88) or has sustained any injury to a leg, for example, which might flare up at a later date.
- Be familiar with his habits -- does he eat his food readily, what is the normal consistency of his droppings and how many piles a day, does he lie down during the day or commonly rest a hind leg when standing?

- His mucous membranes (the tissues behind the eyelids around the eyes and the gums in the mouth) should be salmon pink in colour – if they are very white this may indicate anaemia (a condition caused by a lack of red blood cells that leads to feelings of tiredness). A yellow tinge could signify liver damage, perhaps due to poisoning.

▶ **Pulse/Heart Rate:** At rest a horse's heart rate should be between 30 and 40 beats per minute. It can be taken by pressing a finger on any artery, but is commonly taken under the horse's jaw.

◀ **Temperature:** The normal temperature of a horse or pony is 38°C (100°F). A horse's temperature is usually taken by inserting the end of a thermometer about 4cm (1.75in) inside the rectum and holding it against the side of the bowel wall for about a minute.

◀ **Respiration:** This is the number of breaths a horse takes per minute. It should be between eight and 12 breaths in a resting horse, but will increase after exercise. You can count the breaths by watching the sides of the horse expand and fall as the diaphragm moves.

◀ **Hydration:** In a healthy horse, if you pinch the skin of the neck or shoulder between your fingers then release it, it should spring back flat quickly. If it is slow to flatten, this may be a sign of dehydration meaning that your pony has been deprived of water somehow.

▲ **A horse's pulse** *can be felt by locating the artery under the jaw, in the fetlock joint or in the girth area.*

TIP Keep a diary of the date and type of ailments – perhaps your mare is moody every three weeks when she is in season. It will help you to foresee problems.

HEALTH CHECK BEFORE RIDING

Is he alert and attentive and pleased to see you?

Is there any discharge from his muzzle or does he have dull, weepy eyes?

Are his eyes bright and clear?

Does he seem sullen and disinterested or bad-tempered towards you?

Are the mucous membranes around his eyes, nostrils and gums a salmon-pink colour?

Does he seem agitated, uncomfortable or distressed?

Does his posture indicate he is sound?

Is he shifting his weight, resting his legs, head-shaking or generally looking unsettled or uncomfortable?

 Do not think of riding until you have investigated the cause of the problem

 He appears to be healthy and happy so continue

- **Check body visually** Check body and limbs for cuts, puncture wounds, bites, sores, girth galls, over-reach grazes, mud fever etc. Check legs are not puffy or swollen. Pick out hooves and check for excessive heat in them.
- **Check tack** Check the fit of all tack and its positioning. Make sure all surfaces in contact with the skin are free of grease and mud which could cause chafing.
- **Tighten girth straps gradually and check bit** Check positioning of bit in the mouth. Does the horse seem comfortable with it or could there be a problem? Check for sores or cuts in the mouth.
- **Flex the horse before mounting** Stretch out forelegs to eliminate pinching from the girth. Lead the horse in a small circle, to the left and to the right to allow him to feel the tack and loosen up.
- **Mount slowly** Ideally mount from a mounting block and lower your weight gently into the saddle.
- **Warm up slowly** Begin riding at a walk for a minimum of five minutes. Start on a loose rein to allow him to stretch out. He should be happy and interested in his work.

Recognising & treating common ailments

Call your vet immediately if there is:

- Heavy bleeding
- Severe pain. Obvious signs of distress include groaning, violent rolling, eyes rolling, straining
- Sudden lameness or inability to move willingly
- A foreign body puncturing or embedded in the skin, such as a piece of wire
- Breathing difficulty
- Joint oil (a yellowish fluid) leaking from the wound
- An exposed bone

Keep a close eye on your horse and arrange for the vet to call as soon as possible if there is:

- A cut or puncture wound that has not caused lameness but may require flushing out or stitching
- Lameness, although the horse is able to walk
- Diarrhoea or loss of appetite
- Mild colic (although this may pass before the vet arrives)
- Abnormal behaviour, staggering or moving awkwardly, unusual aggression or hypersensitive behaviour
- Lumps or swellings or foul-smelling areas
- Recurrent coughing or discharge from the nose

COMMON AILMENTS TO BE AWARE OF –
COLIC

Colic is a general term to describe stomach pain. It could be caused by a build up of gas, worm damage or compaction of food somewhere in the intestine causing a blockage, or a twist or dislodgement of part of the intestine. In severe cases the horse will require emergency surgery for any chance of survival.

The symptoms of a horse or pony with colic are that it will appear uncomfortable – it may turn round and nudge or kick at its tummy, repeatedly try to roll and grunt or groan. If it is suffering from over-indulgence caused by eating too much or too quickly, it may be possible to walk the animal around to try to get the stomach and digestive system moving and allow the pain to subside. In all but the mildest cases, a vet should be called immediately as he may need to administer a drench (medicine given in liquid form) or muscle relaxants or even refer the horse to a hospital for surgery.

LAMINITIS/FOUNDER

This is unfortunately a **very** common problem with ponies. The laminae are sensitive tissues inside the hoof wall that cover the pedal bone. Any inflammation here will cause great pain, especially if the pedal bone has rotated too. In severe cases it can even push through the sole of the foot. A laminitic pony will look in a sorry state as he tries to alleviate the pain in his feet by leaning back in an attempt to take the weight off the toes of the hoof. Both front feet and hind feet can be affected, but usually it is confined to the front feet.

In the wild ponies have to walk many miles each day in search of food, but when they live with us, they usually enjoy a more pampered domestic lifestyle with

TIP If your horse's legs are painful with mud fever, there are proprietary herbal remedies that can be fed to help them heal without you needing to touch them.

▶ **The pain from** *a lame front leg can cause a horse to lift his head when walking as he tries to ease his weight off the bad leg.*

▶ **By contrast,** *a horse may lower his head if he is feeling pain in the hindleg as he transfers weight onto his front legs.*

▶ **Horses with laminitis** *stand with their weight on the heels of the affected hooves to relieve the pain experienced in the front of the hoof.*

▶ **A tired horse** *is more prone to injury and a damaged ligament can mean months off work.*

▶▶ **Applying petroleum jelly** *to dry, clean legs will act as a preventative barrier against mud fever.*

much less exercise and plentiful good grazing/hard feed simply given to them. This can often cause an imbalance, triggering an attack. Working a horse on hard ground can also be a cause. However, too much rich grass is far and away the most common culprit.

If you suspect laminitis, call the vet immediately and in the meantime remove your pony from pasture and put him in a stable with a nice thick bed (shavings are best as they help to support the soles of the feet).

MUD FEVER

If you notice hard crusty lumps of hair or scabs around the pasterns and heels of your pony, then it is likely he has mud fever. It is not actually a 'fever' but a bacterial infection. It mainly occurs if horses or ponies are left in muddy conditions in which the bacteria thrive.

When your pony is clean and dry, before he goes out in the field, protect his heels with a layer of petroleum jelly to act as a waterproofing barrier against the mud. If he does get plastered in mud, hose this off and dry his legs with a towel before putting him away. There are also 'turnout socks' on the market now which act like wellington boots for your horse!

The scabs will be hard and sore but once a week wrap a hot wet flannel around the pastern and leave it in place for five minutes. The warmth will help the scabs to soften and you may be able to wipe some of them away. Dispose of all the cloths and scabs carefully so the bacteria will not be spread. Treatment is made easier if the animal is treated by adding herbal supplements to the feed which are designed to support the body in fighting the bacteria.

Recognising & treating common ailments

THRUSH

If you pick out your pony's hoof and are faced with a foul smell and possible discharge or if the frog appears to have loose edges (sometimes tinged grey or black), then this is probably an infection of the hoof called thrush. This is often caused by a pony standing for long periods in

wet conditions or in wet bedding, or if mud has not being picked out of the hoof regularly.

You will need to treat the area with an antiseptic spray and call your farrier who should trim back the frog to healthy tissue.

RAIN SCALD

This has similar symptoms to those of mud fever but it found predominantly along the length of the horse's back. Clumps of hair fall out and scabs may form when infection has taken hold. The cause is simply lack of protection from the elements and it is usually caused by prolonged periods of rain saturating the horse's coat.

Thoroughly wash the horse with an antibacterial shampoo, feed a supplement to improve hair and skin condition and use a rug on the horse in wet weather. Nowadays there are different thicknesses of rugs (*above*)

available on the market so it is possible just to provide a rain sheet in milder conditions without risking the horse becoming overheated.

LICE AND MITES

If you notice your horse itching and scratching his neck, mane or even the feathers on his legs, it is worth investigating if he has an infestation of lice or mites. These creatures are especially attracted to thick coats and a particularly scurfy coat is often a sign of a problem. Ponies rub these itchy areas which can cause bald patches

and a tatty-looking mane. There are powders and lotions which can be applied to kill the infestation or application of a 'spot on' flea treatment as prescribed to dogs can also be a very effective cure.

SWEET ITCH

Some animals are particularly sensitive to biting flies and midges and suffer an allergic reaction to the saliva of the biting flies. The result is that the areas (mainly the mane and tail) are extremely itchy and the horse tries to relieve the itch by rubbing and scratching the areas, causing bald patches and broken mane and tail hairs.

Soothing lotions can be applied to counter the itch/scratch cycle but prevention is better than cure – and manes and tails take many months to grow! In warm weather (and particularly if your horse is kept near a stream or other water course where midges thrive), spray your horse or pony with fly repellent, twice a day if

TIP A good antibacterial solution can be used for a multitude of purposes – from curing an itchy, scurfy coat to disinfecting the stable.

▲ **Constant scratching** *could be a sign of mites.*

▶ **Breathing problems** *can be caused by dust.*

necessary. Sponge down or hose off your pony if he is hot after a ride as a sweaty horse will attract midges like bees to honey, then re-apply more fly repellent.

COUGHS/COPD

Some horses and ponies are more sensitive to contaminants in the air than others and can suffer from breathing problems. Bedding and hay often contains particles of dust, spores and mould which can trigger a repetitive cough or escalate into a form of asthma called COPD (Chronic Obstructive Pulmonary Disease). The lungs can become damaged and the poor animal has great difficulty breathing deeply enough to get adequate oxygen. You can sometimes see a 'heave line' where the pony has strained to breathe.

Once the horse has contracted COPD, he will have to be kept away from anything that could irritate and inflame the breathing passages. Affected ponies benefit from being turned out on grass. If kept inside, careful management is essential to ensure the provision of dust-free bedding. Feed only haylage or soaked hay to minimise the transmission of dust, moulds and spores that are often found in hay and straw.

Horrendous Hooves
Hooves are healthiest when their moisture content is kept more or less constant. Brittle hooves can be caused by the sudden change from a wet field to a dry bed of shavings.

First aid

If you own or care for a pony, a well stocked first aid kit is essential. You never know when you might need to attend to some injury or illness, and it's sensible to have the basic remedies and materials readily to hand. Remember also to take it in the trailer or lorry when you go to a show.

Your first aid kit should contain –

Thermometer 1: For checking the pony's temperature.

Dressings/gauze pads 2: To cover and protect wounds without sticking.

Gamgee padding 3: Used between dressings and bandages for support without causing pressure points.

Poultice pads 4: Can be cut to size and soaked in hot water to help treat hoof abscesses.

Roll of cotton wool 5: Used wet for cleaning wounds or as a bandage padding (not suitable as a dressing direct on a wound as fibres tend to stick to the wound).

Crepe elastic bandage 6: For use over padding for support and protection. Modern bandages stick to themselves for easy application.

Antibiotic spray 7: Helps prevent infection and you can apply a spray without needing to touch the wound.

Scissors 8: For cutting dressings to size (use ones with rounded ends).

Adhesive tape 9: For holding dressings and poultices in place.

Iodine or salt 10: Either can be added to water to make a solution for flushing wounds clean.

Wound powder 11: Prevents infection entering a wound, useful on a small nick that cannot be bandaged. But do not use if you have called the vet as it will hinder his examination.

Tweezers 12: To remove splinters, thorns etc.

Vaseline/petroleum jelly 13: To protect areas prone to chafing (e.g. girth galls) and to lubricate the thermometer before it is inserted.

Disposable gloves 14: Useful when applying ointments and to prevent infection passing from your hands into a wound.

Have a notice or blackboard clearly visible in the yard or tackroom that displays useful telephone numbers including those of your vet and farrier just in case someone needs to contact them urgently in your absence.

HOW TO DEAL WITH MINOR INJURIES

It is best to practise bandaging a leg while your horse is uninjured – both you and he will be calm and you can develop your skills in an unpressurised situation. Then, if he does get a cut, you will feel more confident that you will be able to cope. Remember if you have any doubts about the severity of the wound, then call your vet. Only bandage small wounds which are not near any joints; otherwise seek professional advice.

TIP Use a solution of 1 teaspoon salt to one pint (600ml) of water or a bottled wound wash to clean wounds. Never use undiluted antiseptic as this may burn exposed flesh.

Remember: Never use cotton wool as a dressing directly onto the wound or the fibres will stick to it. Cotton wool can be used to clean the wound provided it is wet or positioned behind a dressing as padding.

HOW TO BANDAGE A LEG WOUND

1. Flush out the wound with saline or iodine solution or a specialist wound wash. Apply a healing antiseptic wound gel (omit this if the vet is coming to examine the horse).
2. Cover the wound with a non-stick dressing pad.
3. Use a large piece of absorbent wadding or gamgee (absorbent cushioned padding for leg support and protection) behind this to absorb any discharge and to help support the limb and reduce swelling.
4. Apply a stretch bandage to hold everything in place. This can either be cohesive which will stick to itself, or a cotton bandage tied around the limb and then secured with tape. Leave a gap in the bandage to allow the joint to flex.
5. Bandage the opposite leg just with gamgee and an elastic bandage to help support it -- your pony will put more weight on it to avoid using the injured leg!

Index

Note: Page numbers set in *italic type* refer to captions to pictures; page numbers set in **bold type** indicate the main subject reference.

Index and Picture Credits

Picture Credits